Training the Teacher as a Champion

By Joseph K. Hasenstab and Connie Corcoran Wilson

Performance Learning Systems, inc.
Nevada City, California 95959

Published by
Performance Learning Systems, inc.
224 Church Street
Nevada City, California 95959

Copyright ©1989 by Performance Learning Systems
Designed by Donna Burke

ISBN 0-9621766-0-5

Printed in the United States.

Table of Contents

END OF BOOK

Dedication

*T*his book is dedicated to my lifelong "big brother," friend and mentor, Cornelius C. Rose, Jr.

Neil and I worked together as lifeguards in the late fifties. He was in law school; I was yet to graduate from high school. As in any mentoring situation, where the older coaches the younger, he helped me gain thinking skills and confidence.

When I was looking for new challenges, he financed Performance Learning Systems. Through its concept and development years he has given PLS thousands of hours of consultation and counsel, never once taking a penny. He shrugs and says, "I want to do it because I want to give something back to education."

A Phi Beta Kappa at Colgate University, Neil earned an LLB from New York University, a Master of Arts degree from Columbia and did additional graduate work at several universities. For twenty years he pursued a career as a professional "deal maker," creating, buying and selling businesses. While he could simply clip coupons from prior ventures, he believes in the dignity of our vision. In helping us he has helped teachers help children be "everything they can be."

As long as I can remember, he has always asked the right question and started the right analysis. Most important, he gave each of us the courage to *do.*

When I talk of mentoring and coaching, the model of "how to" is C.C. Rose — my mentor for 35 years.

Acknowledgements

I want to give my personal thanks to the many, many people who helped develop this book by giving generously of their expertise in the field of education, contributing their reactions and keeping a sharp eye out for supporting material, and sometimes contradicting material. Their input helped make this a more balanced, more accurate statement of what education needs today.

And thanks to Don Baumgart, a writer with an excellent sense of a tight, well-spoken message, for polishing the later versions.

And, my deep thanks to all the staff at Performance Learning Systems for their help and support in creating this book.

Thanks to the many kind souls who gave of their time and knowledge to read the semi-final draft and give me their comments. They include:

J.W. Atkinson	Ontario Public School Teachers' Federation
Beverly Boomsma	Performance Learning Systems
Louise E. Dieterle	University of Northern Illinois
Charles A. Kadel	Pennsylvania Cumberland Valley School District
Marcia Mann	University of South Florida
D.P. Magann	Superintendent, Alachua County Schools, Florida
Charles J. Santelli	New York State United Teachers
Tom Willette	New York State United Teachers

Thanks to my wife Geraldine for her constant support. Any partner who survives the writing of a book deserves a medal.

Last and foremost, my unending thanks to the teachers who, by their renewed enthusiasm for leading our children into learning, have told me again and again that I am on the right track.

—Joe Hasenstab

We also want to thank the many authors whose works are quoted in this book:

"A Guide for Assessing Public Issues: Remember to Do It on Four Levels." Copyright 1986, Charley Reese & The Orlando Sentinel.

"A Nation Prepared: Teachers for the 21st Century." Copyright 1986, Carnegie Forum on Education and the Economy.

"A.S.C.D. Yearbook" Copyright 1986, Association for Supervision and Curriculum Development.

"Better Teachers for the Year 2000: A Proposal for the Structural Reform of Teacher Education." Copyright 1984, David L. Clark.

"Can Educational Research Inform Educational Practice?" Copyright 1984, Elliot W. Eisner.

"Changing Teacher Practices: Proceedings of a National Conference." Copyright 1982, Maria E. Defino and Heather Carter.

"Cost Effectiveness: A Primer." Copyright 1983, Henry M. Levin.

"Collegiality May Be the Password to Effective Inservice Programs." Copyright 1982, Wynn DeBevoise.

"Critical Attributes of a Staff Development Program to Increase Instructional Effectiveness." Copyright 1986, Madeline Hunter and Doug Russell.

"Education Reform: A Managerial Agenda." Copyright 1986, Samuel B. Bacharach and Sharon C. Conley.

"Language Disability in Men of Eminence." Copyright 1971, Lloyd J. Thompson.

"Laughter: It's Medicine for the Mind and Body." Copyright 1985, D.J. Moore.

"Learning Communities for Curriculum and Staff Development." Copyright, 1986, Anne Wescott Dodd.

"Let's Admit We Can't Train Teachers — and Ask for Help." Copyright 1983, John F. Newport.

"Mining Good Staff Development Ideas in Business." Copyright 1983, Fred H. Wood.

"On the Expert Teacher." Copyright 1986, David C. Berliner.

"Our Profession, Our Schools: The case for Fundamental Reform." Copyright 1986, Albert Shanker.

"Perceived Changes in Styles of Learning and Thinking (Hemisphericity) Through Direct and Indirect Training." Copyright 1986, Cecil R. Reynolds and E. Paul Torrence.

Introduction

I taught sixth, seventh, eighth, and ninth grades. My first two courses in education as a teacher in 1960 were a curriculum course and a psychology course. The professor gave both courses from exactly the same notes. He gave exactly the same final in both courses. I handed in identical papers and received an "A" in both courses.

I had an empty feeling in the pit of my stomach. "Is this it?" I had discovered the king had no clothes.

It struck me right from the beginning that what I really wanted to learn was "how" to teach...the magical moves that made a difference in kids' lives. And all I was hearing was a lot of history, conclusions, goals, and standards. It kept occurring to me again and again that there were skill and performance patterns that particularly good teachers used. What I wanted, what I needed to become a good teacher, was yet to be available.

I was in the profession for about ten years. My teaching years were beautiful years. I loved teaching. And more than ever, I love and have a zest for helping people be everything they can be — to do the magic of teaching.

Then, for several years I applied a simple notion to other fields. **The notion was that successful people *do*. Spectators write, doers do. My notion was, if you want to find out what works, ask a successful doer.**

I analyzed the performance moves of outstanding practitioners as it applied to negotiators and detectives. I was interested in the building blocks — what word structures, what tonality and body language worked.

From those investigations the typical response from negotiators, detectives, and teachers was, "I don't know what makes me successful, I just do it with a gut feeling." And yet, they had very successful, complex, intuitive moves that made them different from other people — and with additional probing a flood of common skills and strategies emerged.

The experts in a specific field have two things in common. The first thing is a greater width of skills. They have more moves in their repertoires. And, they have a second common quality. Like a chess player they see the moves deeper than the average person. The more highly honed the skills, the deeper they see. My basic approach was to define the skills they used, and train those skills.

Using that approach, I designed two courses. Verbal Skills in Negotiation trained more than 200,000 teacher negotiators over 15 years. Criminal Investigation for the New York Police Department lasted until the Miranda Decision.

When I started Project T.E.A.C.H., my entry into teacher education, I was met with suspicion at best. I tried to get teacher organizations, state education departments and foundations to fund the research and design. I found myself alone. I came to a fundamental decision to put my money and my best friend's money where my mouth was. I put everything on the line, and it was the best decision I ever made.

In a relatively short period of seven months of interviewing teachers we broke the code, and the only thing that millions of dollars of research has proved in the past 15 years is that we were correct...*that the genius of the teaching profession is in the performing artist.*

If the researchers had talked to teachers instead of doing check-mark research, they would have learned what we learned 15 years ago: If you want to find out what works, build a composite of the skill and performance patterns of experts and put that in a training design that teaches what works.

When the training design was completed, we trained excellent teachers to instruct it. So we were the first to analyze the superstars' moves in teaching, and first to use superstars as educators of teachers. We now have 23 firsts in teacher education; some significant, some technical.

So many books in the teacher education field are written by spectators and journalists. Be comfortable that you are reading a book written by a person who slugged it out in the trenches for our clients and ourselves, learning along the way the intricacies of how decisions are made for educators. The number of teachers trained by Performance Learning Systems has increased ten times in the past seven years in a declining teacher education market. We and our client groups together are the largest provider (in consortium) in North America, training 25,000 teachers in 1987.

In the early years our training was like Edison going up against the gas lamp lobby. Now we find it an advantage to our clients that we are a private sector training group, because it removes us from the whims of hierarchical, sometimes political, decision making. We are unique in our freedom to concern ourselves with only one thing: What works in teacher education, and applying it. The message I'm conveying here, and in the rest of this book, is just this: "Here it is, and it works!"

We are pleased to be ahead of the times in education when we see our programs fit the calls for action coming from concerned bodies like the Holmes Group, which is characterized as a group of conservative "old boy" education research institutions. It's really fun to watch their proposals take the form of suggestions to their institutions that we as a group have already accomplished and have institutionalized. (We also fit the radical changes described as needed by the Carnegie Report, which had representatives of the two main teacher organizations on its task force.) When major voices in education begin calling for the moves we began training 15 years ago, we can allow ourselves to gloat a bit.

In this book you will find my best attempt to describe today's crucial crossroads in education, and what I feel are the best possible solutions. While I define some of the problems, this book is different because it gives you the solutions that have worked for teachers.

Joseph K. Hasenstab

Chapter 1   The Five-Year Window

"We must take the current when it serves, or lose our ventures."—Shakespeare, Julius Caesar

I have to be candid; I think the approach documented in this book is the only honest approach to training teachers. Train them as performing artists—train them in the workplace — train them by the best teaching models we have, and train them as if we assume they are champions.

We have before us right now the opportunity to change and vastly improve the quality of education our children will receive. These few critical years, used wisely, can enable us to effect changes that will produce capable, educated adults whose chances of success and meaningful contribution to society have been greatly enhanced by our timely action.

We are in a five-year window of time, when the majority of teachers and teacher educators will be retiring. One projection suggests that by the fall of 1993 an additional 1.65 million public and private elementary and secondary school teachers will be needed as teachers leave the profession or retire. That's more than two-thirds of the 2.4 million teachers in classrooms today.[1] Other projections predict a 50 percent turnover.

Therefore, a window of opportunity exists during this five-year period to significantly improve teacher education, thus affecting the staff members who will shape future generations of students. Now is the time when implementation of reform measures will adversely affect the smallest number of people. At this crucial time a sense of responsibility to future generations of students, and the quality of their education, must take precedence over maintaining the status quo. Meaningful reform must be implemented.

A report from the **Holmes Group, which represents education research institutions,** titled "Tomorrow's Teachers" articulated this thought in the spring of 1986:

> ...we have also found ourselves willing to argue for
> radical improvements that most of us would have

dismissed as impractical just a few years ago. We have decided that we must work for the changes that we believe to be right, rather than those we know can succeed. Much is at stake, for American students' performance will not improve much if the quality of teaching is not improved. And teaching will not improve much without dramatic improvements in teacher education.[2]

While in agreement with The Holmes Group that "reforming professional teacher preparation requires the full participation of practicing teachers and teacher educators" and that "changes of this sort are easier to describe than to carry off,"[3] the point upon which all of us involved in education must agree is this: We are the future. The buck stops here!

This window of opportunity will not remain open forever. Today, when more highly paid veteran teachers are retiring, is the time to utilize the money saved through teacher attrition to give skill training to all teachers. A veteran teacher, on the average, costs twice as much as a novice teacher; we must take the dollar difference realized during this five-year span and make a dynamic difference.

The following actions need to be taken.

1. Train the Generic Performing Moves

The generic skills are a teacher's tools. The most creative architect in the world, in the end, relies on saws, hammers, and nails to build the house of his loftiest visions.

The Holmes Group report says:

"If teaching is to be recognized as a discipline, it must be conceived not in terms of duties and roles, but in terms of the generic skills and knowledge that transcend any given setting."[4]

The constant dedication of the educator to perfecting the fundamentals is vital to the success of the teaching enterprise — the same dedication pilots, ballet dancers, actors, and athletes bring to their specialties.

These skills can be trained to the first level of internalization in approximately 200 hours, including 20 to 60 hours of personalized coaching.

Concern for the absence of this training can be seen in the Holmes Group report, evident in statements such as these:

> Providing prospective teachers with strong subject matter knowledge does not equip them with the understanding or skill necessary to teach that knowledge to someone else.[5]

Or, as in this statement,

> Reforming the education of teachers depends upon engaging in the complex work of identifying the knowledge base for competent teaching, and developing the content and strategies whereby it is imparted.[6]

The report continues,

> It takes training, for example, to wait more than a few seconds for pupils to answer a question before filling the silence with elaborative comments that disrupt the students' thinking. It takes training to increase the higher order questions a teacher asks; to decrease the preponderance of teacher talk; to provide advanced organizers, plans, and clear directions, to give teachers the cognitive resources to make pedagogical decisions and to manage productively the hundreds of distinct interactions they will have with pupils each day.[7]

The Holmes Group report brings out the need for the teaching of classroom handling techniques in college education courses, saying:

> Instructing learners in groups and managing numbers of students in confined spaces calls for yet another set of skills that go well beyond keeping order.[8]

"Tomorrow's Teachers" concludes,

> The academic pedagogical studies available in colleges of education routinely fail to develop such essential professional knowledge, skills, and dispositions of the teachers they prepare.[9] From the earlier discussion it should be obvious that

competent, responsible teachers must possess far more than subject matter knowledge.[10]

This need for the teaching of the hands-on skills of effective classroom handling was articulated much earlier than The Holmes Group report by N.L. Gage of Stanford University, who expressed it this way:

We hear that teacher education courses are irrelevant, too theoretical. The courses are full of material about learners and learning when prospective teachers want to know about teachers and teaching. The courses tell about the history, philosophy, sociology, and psychology of education, when prospective teachers want to know how they should teach. The courses give future teachers knowledge of the subject matter to be taught, when prospective teachers may already know far more about a subject than they will ever need in teaching third-graders or even 12th-graders.

The evidence that knowledge of a subject is not enough to make a teacher is plain to anyone who has ever seen a PhD in mathematics thoroughly confuse a freshman calculus course — or the holder of a Bachelor's degree obfuscate the past tense in teaching third-grade reading. Thus generations of teacher education students have been given inadequate grounding in **how** to teach. They have not been taught **how** to organize a course, **how** to plan a lesson, **how** to manage a class, **how** to give an explanation, **how** to arouse interest and motivation, **how** to ask various kinds of questions, **how** to react to students' responses, **how** to avoid unfair biases in interacting with students — in short, **how** to teach.[11]

In a 1983 study David K. Cohen of Holmes Group member Michigan State University, expressed the opinion that teachers must be taught how to teach when he said, "they [teachers] must marry technical knowledge with interactive skills,"[12] and stated that "interactive skill and knowledge is thus seen as a precondition for the exercise of technical competence."[13]

In regard to the generic skills of teaching, a leading authority in the field of teacher education, Madeline Hunter of the University of California at Los Angeles, has written:

Based on the assumption that there now exists a science which undergirds the art of teaching, teacher development programs need to be constituted so they create a foundation of cause-effect relationships which are not limited to any one content area, learner or situation but which are useful in all educational decisions and applicable to any educational endeavor.[14]

Guaranteeing that teachers are taught the generic skills necessary to become effective teachers is the best way to produce good teachers. For far too long we have urged teachers to do this or that, achieve this or that abstract goal in the classroom without telling them how. The expert, instructing the classroom teacher, might say, "Your students need to increase their time on task." That abstract advice needs to be turned into concrete advice that will yield educational gains in the classroom.

Each goal — whether increasing time on task, which is more than 40 skill and performance patterns, or achieving some other outcome — **must be spelled out in terms of skill and performance patterns**, i.e., what the teacher must do, including word structures, tonality, and body language, to achieve the desired objective. Give teachers the performing moves for classroom scenarios. Until teacher educators have concrete steps that outline exactly how a teacher "gets from here to there" in the classroom, instructions like "increase your students' time on task" will be worthless. Only when teachers give as much energy to mastering the all-important "tricks of the trade" that comprise the generic teaching skills as they devote to mastering the subject matter of their chosen fields will they truly learn how to teach.

2. Train Everyone in the Same Performing Language

The training must include all licensed personnel within the district, including the administrators. Everyone must possess a common vocabulary and recognize superior execution of practices.[15,16]

As a company official said in an NCR training program,

Trainees often return from training to find a manager who does not understand or support the new procedures or skills that have been learned....Educators, especially superintendents, must place higher priority on teacher development if we are to have quality educators.... Administrators need to model, through visible involvement in ongoing professional growth experiences, the importance they place on teacher development.[17]

3. Train and Coach Teachers in the Workplace

By making the training convenient and by lessening the impact on teachers' personal time, the concept of Long-Term Teacher Development can be made acceptable to the working teacher. Training must be transformed from an esoteric teacher burden that takes valuable time "away from teaching," to valuable sound practices that make teaching exciting.

Teacher education belongs in the workplace. Training must occur during the day, and must be accorded the same amenities as in private sector management training.

As Madeline Hunter said,

> Ideally, inservice is conducted during the work day. If it is done after school or on non-work days, there should be some acknowledgement of the extra time and effort involved....A frequently neglected but essential aspect of the time demands of 'when' is the necessity for systematic follow-up observations of the teachers', administrators' and district leaders' implementation of the inservice content. These observations should be followed by prescriptive feedback which is either reinforcing or remediating....The time required for observation and feedback [coaching] is one of the most costly inservice factors but is essential to a successful program.[18]

Why must teachers be trained in the generic performing moves in schools? For the same reason pro quarterbacks are trained on the playing field: because it is a hands-on profession.

4. Train Teachers with the Best Models of Good Teaching

Educators of teachers must model the most effective teaching practices, implementing proven training designs.

Teachers want concrete, specific solutions from crackerjack, upbeat, positive, warm, clear communicators who successfully model sound practices as they teach sound practices.

"Beginning teachers are more influenced by the models of teaching they have seen in their own teachers and professors than by the information presented to them in methods classes. In their own classrooms, teachers often teach as their teachers did. The power of teaching by example cannot be overestimated, and it must play a role in curriculum and teacher development."[19]

Teacher educators must be chosen from the best of teachers, must model the most effective teaching practices, and must be able to give demonstration lessons, coach others, and be coached in turn. They must be available as consultants, coaches, and models of effective practices. Modeling proven practice is essential for teacher educators.

The Holmes Group report concurs, saying, "If university faculties are to become more expert educators of teachers, they must make better use of expert teachers in the education of other teachers...."[20] The report recommends that the undergraduate curriculum be sharply revised so that "future teachers can study the subjects they will teach with instructors who model fine teaching and who understand the pedagogy of their material." [21]

5. Reward Teachers for Their Actions

Teachers want rewards for learning to teach well...not for sitting in classes and writing papers. Teachers would prefer to demonstrate their execution of proficiencies in the classroom, if the judgment of sound teaching practices is done by experts from the profession. The reward system, intrinsic and extrinsic, should match the desires, expectations, and needs of educators.

Educators simply require the same TLC in the development of their professional aspirations as their students require. Teachers are expected to show genuine concern for their students as individuals; all teachers ask is similar treatment from the system.

The future of education depends very heavily on making teaching a profession and giving teachers more control over their environment.[22] No one has really asked educators the question, "If you entered teaching again, what rewards would you find valuable?"

Educators value the intrinsic rewards of teaching. These rewards include a positive school environment, amenities, and honest listening by the district concerning problems and their solutions.

Albert Shanker, President of the American Federation of Teachers, has noted, "The future of education depends very heavily on making teaching a profession and giving teachers a modicum of control over their environment."[23] Shanker's thesis is seconded by the Holmes Group's statement:

> But none of the reform proposals has addressed the central issue in the improvement of teaching — the professional stature of teachers. Until this is addressed, we will continue to attempt educational reform by telling teachers what to do, rather than empowering them to do what is necessary....Reform advocates have never fully appreciated the fact that the problems of teacher education mirror society's failure to treat teaching as a profession. [24]

Now is the time for teachers and administrators and teacher educators with their representatives to discuss the merits of a new system of teacher training with school boards, state departments, and legislative bodies. Now is the time to redefine specifically the mission of teacher education and the intrinsic and extrinsic rewards necessary to attract and retain the most capable people to the profession. Shanker adds:

> There is going to be a talent shortage in this country; and given the increased demand for talent by new and revamped industries and by other agencies of government, there is very little chance that public education will get enough high-caliber career teachers. The demographics are against us....I am convinced that we will not attract the best and the brightest who are graduating today if teachers continue to be treated as they currently are....[25]

To that observation I add these thoughts supporting the need for reform in teacher education: we will only produce the best and the brightest teachers if we do what the major companies and the professional sports teams do — find people with the right attributes, then recruit and train them as champions.

"We can no longer afford the luxury of academic snobbery that has traditionally relegated the education and training of teachers to second class status."[26]

Part of the snobbery is placing emphasis on academic rigor, rather than skill development.

Fundamental to all performing arts are the skill and performance patterns that are trained and coached. Learning to perform is gaining precision and finesse in simple as well as complex elegant moves. This synthesis process is active and dynamic. When we think of competent performers, the quality of their skills and performance patterns leap forward to our senses.

Most teacher training has been an analysis process full of conclusions and standard statements. It is the skillful moves that achieve the standards in the performing arts. Skillful moves are the "how" to achieve desirable conclusions.

This book is a positive hopeful, statement "how" teachers can be trained as champion performers.

The lyrics to a popular George Benson song, re-recorded by Whitney Houston, begins, "I believe the children are our future; teach them well and let them lead the way. Show them all the beauty they possess inside; give them a sense of pride to make it easier."

Our reform credo, paraphrasing those lyrics, might be expressed this way: Show teachers the beauty of their profession. Give them a sense of pride in their work and proper training to make that work easier. I believe our teachers shape the future. Teach teachers well; let them lead the way.

The greatest thrill in teaching is developing students who exceed us. The greatest joy in teaching is contributing to the growth of learners so the results exceed our expectations and theirs. The reward of teaching is making differences in people's lives. The craft of teaching is applying the magical moves that compose those differences.

The window is open. Before it closes, will we take a bold look at the future...or will we turn our backs on the spectacular view? The choice is ours.

Chapter 2 | History of Higher Teacher Education

"Change takes place no matter what deters it....there must be measured, laborious preparation for change to avoid chaos."—Plato

*T*he Way We Remember the "Credit Rush"

To create a better way of training teachers, we first have to know what exists and how it came to be.

The current higher education system for teachers, the Master's and 60-hour incentive plan, was started in the 1950s and 1960s to attract people to the teaching profession.

Collective bargaining enhanced the incentive plan by increasing future rewards. School boards in those years, with a majority of young teachers at the bottom of the salary scale, mortgaged future school boards with incentive plans that rewarded teachers who went back to college and accumulated graduate education credits.

I remember very well in the pre-negotiations "collective begging" days, the school board would put up a chart showing where we would be with years of service and graduate degrees. We who remember know that those school boards didn't understand the implications of a "credit rush." Teachers rushed to get advanced college course credits solely for reasons of salary advancement. It had little to do with learning to become better teachers.

The colleges and universities welcomed the teacher tuition and the state subsidies because training teachers was cheap and provided revenue for the institution to use elsewhere. For the teacher it was attend, write a paper, and move up on the salary scale.

While statistics are not available to show how many courses school districts have purchased in the past 35 years through incentives and tuition rebates, the profit center was a money machine that Rockefeller would envy.

While there is a range of variability, universities receive about $400-$800 per enrollment in 1988 dollars through tuition and tax subsidies. Historically, they have kept two-thirds and passed along one-third to the education department, making a $260-$525 profit per enrollment. Multiplying the number of teacher enrollments for 35 years times $260-$525 per enrollment is mega-bucks. Millions of teachers received college course tuition reimbursement and substantial salary incentives for hundreds of billions of dollars over their teaching careers. The universities have a regulated monopoly on teacher education. Two of every three dollars is profit, no guarantee, no warranty; just the power of a powerful incentive system keeps it a rolling windfall.

In many cases, the reason teachers drive to college campuses rather than the university coming to district sites is that the university as a whole is receiving state subsidies (Full Time Equivalencies, or FTEs) for university enrollment on-campus with far lesser FTEs for off-campus work. This caused teacher education to become campus based rather than field based even though all the research on internalization of sound practice demands field-based training of teachers.

Are educators or society getting their money's worth? By anyone's standards, the answer is no.

In the fifties and sixties, most state colleges were almost exclusively teacher education schools. Because teaching teachers was cheap, large surpluses were built up from teacher fees and the state/provincial subsidies for each enrollment. This supply of money was used in the sixties to build new college facilities and to support other non-teacher education programs on campuses across the land. From the mid-fifties through the mid-seventies teacher education became the primary profit center for many colleges and universities.

While teacher education is a money machine for some, for the local school districts it became an acute fiscal problem. Teachers followed the district's incentive plans: "Stay, get tenure, get credits, and we'll double your salary in 13 years."

In the early seventies, when teachers matured to the top of the salary guides instituted by the school boards of the fifties and sixties, a fiscal crisis produced a reduction in force, which meant that few new teachers were hired for more than a decade. The financial crisis, coupled with a lack of raises during recessions, caused a 15% reduction in real income for teachers between 1971 and 1981.

Consider what each hour of college teacher training attendance costs the school district over 30 years. One local salary guide has a $10,000 difference between the Bachelor's degree rate and the Master's degree plus 60 rate. Over 30 years, $10,000 a year, this represents a district cost of $300,000. For the teacher, a Master's degree plus 60 hours equals 30 courses, each having 40 in-class hours, a total of 1,200 hours. Dividing $300,000 by 1,200 in-class hours, the teacher's 30-year reward is $250 for each hour of class attendance.

For the school board the question must be: "Was each hour of teacher attendance in class worth $250?" The school board, enmeshed by past promises, gambled incorrectly that the payoff for this pot of gold would be a better teacher.

I certainly believe teachers should get all the money they deserve in this important and vital profession. I do think teachers and teacher educators are shortchanged in that tax money is paid to universities, not to university *education* departments. Another short change was that the goal of improving teacher performance was never stated or agreed to by the universities.

In Pursuit of Academic Pursuit?

Education research has not shown that teacher education as an "academic pursuit" makes any difference in teacher performance in the classroom. The research does show that as teachers pass the decade mark in experience their performance drops. I am not suggesting that there is a causal relationship between accumulating credits and decreases in performance. I do suggest that the accumulation of college and university credits is not improving teacher performance.

It is interesting to note that, with all the millions of dollars spent on education research, and the tens of thousands of doctoral dissertations that have been successfully defended, not one deals with this basic issue: Does the money spent on these graduate education programs and incentives produce a better and/or more competent teacher?

Derek C. Bok, President of Harvard University, went on record saying that schools of education have a "marginal status" in universities. In his 1987 report to Harvard's board of overseers, Bok said schools of education

> ... should strive to exemplify the highest standards of instruction and come forth with challenging new ideas about better methods of instruction, better ways of assessing student progress, better ways of helping those who find it difficult to learn.

Many teachers and principals have been critical of their formal preparation, regarding practical experience as the best way of mastering their craft. Investigators have added to these suspicions by consistently failing to discover any causal connection between the training that teachers receive and their subsequent record in raising the achievement levels of their students.

Unless the [education] faculty exemplifies superior performance in its educational practices, it can hardly be convincing in seeking to inspire students to achieve the highest standards in their own professional careers.[27]

Faced with the current concern over teacher education, many universities have even taken the position that a Master's degree plus 60 hours beyond is only an "academic pursuit" and is not supposed to improve teaching performance. I find that interesting and eye-opening news.

Many university professors rightfully claim that the state education departments and other accrediting agencies have approved and continue to approve their programs which are designed as purely academic pursuits, and that delivering a more competent teacher has never been a stated goal. They also claim that certain non-education programs are more expensive to run than others, and that using teacher education profits to support other university programs is acceptable. I wonder if those who pay the bills agree.

It is worthy to note that out of the Normal Schools of the 1940s and 1950s, came the university system. The original Normal Schools had close and fond relationships with teachers. As Normal Schools became universities, the "how to's" of building a lesson plan, lesson delivery, and teacher wisdom became vocational or nonacademic. The teacher educators who wanted close, intimate relationships with teachers were out-voted by their own philosophical, psychological, and sociological research faculties. These disciplines are intellectual, abstract results whereas Normal School instructors were "hands on" facilitators. Further, teacher education Master's degrees, as a whole, were and still are approved by general faculties of the college, who had and have an "academic rigor bias." The "how to" teacher educators became pre-service practice teaching faculty. This dynamic probably caused the Association of Teacher Educators to form.

Performance Learning Systems (PLS) grew in response to a need by practicing teachers to learn their craft beyond practice teaching — a need abandoned by the universities when Normal Schools became colleges. Lortie, according to Marso and Pigge of Bowling Green University, said, "the teaching profession itself lacks a codified body of knowledge and skills which further complicates a beginning teacher's sudden transition into a complex and demanding profession. He further concluded that *learning by doing* rather than formal training is seen by the profession *as the more important aspect of professional development."* He concluded that the profession was *abandoned* in its highest need area.[28]

When PLS was developing the 160 skill and performance patterns and a codified body of knowledge, we approached universities for graduate credit for our field-based courses to be taught by expert teachers to train sound practices. The reaction was, for the most part, negative. Fortunately, over 91 colleges and universities, and 46 state and provincial teacher organizations (to date) had the courage to recognize that a teacher's performance patterns cause student learning and that internalization of sound practice is more valuable than "talking about" sound practice.

"Academic rigor" in reality is a myth, except to people who require it. Teachers cope with writing papers by either gritting it out or "borrowing" a paper from a friend. In either case, the best readings and lecture can do for practice is 10% internalization. As Joyce and Showers point out in another chapter, 80% internalization of sound practices is possible.

The clue as to why university educators are so focused on educators writing papers is that they themselves are expected to write in a "publish or perish" reward system. I once read over 500 resumes by teacher educators. Fully two-thirds of each resume cited published and unpublished articles. My unscientific hypothesis is that teacher educators use papers as resources for their own published and unpublished writings. Of the 500 plus resumes, only two, in cover letters, alluded to the ability to teach, for which the ad I placed was explicit. When 500 cover letters and resumes allude to academic pursuit, when teaching ability was requested, it's clear what's valued by the academic community. If academics are to believe their own theoretical underpinnings and research, it makes sense that the "rigor" they perform be sound practices as they teach sound practices. Academic rigor, therefore, is giving a "live show" of sound practices so that teachers have something to emulate and practice themselves. The highest form of intellectual achievement is *being* in modus operandi what we say or write.

The problem with generalizations is the exceptions. There are exceptional researchers, theorists, historians, and teachers on college campuses throughout the land. There are caring and loving personnel in education departments who want to be helpful—except the system is handicapping their capabilities and visions to be helpful. I use the valuable resources of the researchers, theorists, and interviews with expert teachers in the identification of skills and development of training designs. I highly respect their work. Yet, I could not have accomplished what I did accomplish in a bureaucracy. Innovation is usually accomplished by individuals and independent groups.

Because we seek 80% internalization, our PLS courses have teachers practice clearly defined skills in class. Through carefully designed inductive experiments (action research) teachers report back in writing and discussion what they learned as a result of practicing a skill 30-40 times. They apply skills to instances and make personalized generalizations.

When a teacher presents a tape recording on classroom questions to their triad and instructor, there is no doubt who did the work. When they are asked in writing, "What differences do you note from your pretape?" and "What changes do you still wish to make?", it has the rigor of moving toward internalization. To achieve a 40% internalization requires the teacher to conscientiously practice a skill 30-40 times. The design solution to encourage internalization is to make the service so personalized that the teacher would feel awkward in not doing the work. That's why instructors respond in a folder every session to the teacher's experiments, and in a separate writing in the folder, to their growth.

When teachers feel this accountability system to both the instructor and the class members, they have something to emulate to their students. Further, when teachers have 30-40 experiences with students, they can make generalizations that correlate to educational research. This model comes from the education research and therefore is a sound practice. Lecture and papers are least effective and are not sound practice, especially when they're done as a modus operandi of non-modeling of sound practice.

Teachers must be able to "read" classroom events. Out of that reading comes the weighing of the next teaching move. This is based on a complex mental process of weighing options (skills) and knowledge (common sense, education research). Next comes the performance stage, that is, doing what was decided.

We've spent two decades looking at the teacher from the eyes of a teacher as he or she faces students, taking full responsibility for the above, whereas "academic pursuit" education is at the knowledge phase. They assume knowledge is where their responsibility stops.

Fundamental to this whole book is the question, is it helpful and valuable for teachers to spend their time sorting their own teaching events, the options and the delivery, or is it more valuable that they read articles and write a footnoted paper?

In many states our teachers have to write these papers to fill the "academic rigor requirement" on top of our research classroom assignments. My questions are, conversely, "Where is the linkage in graduate education to practice?... Where do courses link to teaching events?... Why aren't accrediting agencies asking these fundamental questions?"

The need for a codified language, expert teachers modeling sound practice, and hands-on help in coaching proven requirements of sound practices is a tough advocacy for a private sector company because private sector implies greed to some people, rather than independence to pursue a vision. The vision of PLS is to develop competent teachers through a consortium of interested parties. We are, in effect, textbook publishers taking our share of the responsibility for teacher internalization of sound practice.

The Trend

By the early eighties, there was a reduction of college enrollment by potential teachers due to low teacher retirements and the hiring of very few new employees. However, university teacher education departments held their tenured faculty as enrollments dropped, increasing university costs for teacher education courses. So the money machine in teacher education is at a crossroad as to vision and mission.

In addition, merit pay could have made a serious dent in the pay for credits. The recent growth of National Council of States on Inservice Education and the National Staff

Development Council communicates a growth of state department and district staff development. As an example, NSDC is picking up 300 new members a month.

Educational researchers, philosophers, and psychologists are vital long-term partners with on-the-line educators. Unfortunately, even if they decided to follow the research that the Holmes Group report suggested, they have no real latitude to change their modus operandi. They are victims of their funding sources and accrediting agencies who critique menus, not the meal. Their governing bodies want academic rigor, not an improved teacher. The Bok quote was one of dozens that beat up victims. Teacher education has second-class citizenship on most campuses and that's a crime—because it's our profession.

An Impossible Job?

I believe that salaries are only a part of what is keeping our brightest young people from choosing a teaching career. Teaching has acquired the reputation of being an impossible job. This bad reputation is due to the fact that the kind of training teachers get and how teaching is modeled, does little to support teaching as a profession. Teacher education has second-class citizenship on campuses, to the point where future teachers almost apologize for their choice of profession.

With increasing retirements, we face a struggle to attract quality replacements. Now is the time, before we have a second credit rush by the new teachers who will be arriving in the next few years, to ask some hard questions. Do we want to keep the same incentive system when we know there is no correlation between credits earned and teacher effect on student learning? Or, should we replace it with a system that rewards teachers for internalizing effective skills that do effect student learning?

I mention these historical points because when Judy Lanier of the Holmes Group said, "Apparently the business of teacher education in America *has been a thriving one for higher education,* and even talk about incentives that might disrupt its continuance or increase its costs threatened *those profiting from the status quo,*" she refers to a 40-year profit center that subsidizes paying above guide salaried faculty and programs in biology, physics, engineering, law, business, and medicine.[29] The obvious problem of the Holmes Group document is that the deans who compose the Holmes Group are out-voted internally on reform to build a profession, that is, their own faculties, the business office, and the general faculty.

If the focus had been placed on the development of more proficient teachers beginning in the 1950s, on training proficiency using these significant resources lost to other college programs, the teaching profession would be in much better shape today.

I have to wonder what today's teaching would actually be like if school boards and state education departments had insisted on two things. First, that greater teacher proficiency was the goal of teacher education, and, second, that all teacher education tuition had to be used within the education department.

My notion is that before we make the error of discarding university teacher education and the Master's Plus Incentive System, a total reorganization of teacher education should come about legislatively by interested parties. I would make Colleges of Teacher Education independent units with all FTEs going to the education departments. I would trust professional organizations to select their best and brightest and for them to choose additional public members, perhaps from the Society for Training and Development, to form a Board of Trustees to build a coherent, pragmatic, reliable way to train educators and keep them current.

Basic common sense should prevail. The business of teaching is making the clients everything they can be. The business of teacher education is causing client growth through the improvement of professional practices. Professional practices are improved by skills training to teaching events. An artist can do anything creative after mastering the precision of skills. The same is true of teaching.

If we have the integrity of truth over job security, we will recognize that:

1) Teacher education is grossly underfunded, fragmented, and lacks a clear mission.

2) We have to be trained by our best, proven teachers.

3) We have to pay a proven teacher educator well above current teacher salaries. As it stands, our best teachers can't afford to go from the top of the K-12 guide to the bottom of the university guide.

4) The training of teachers must be attribute driven and personalized as if we are training a performing artist.

5) The training of teachers should include a supportive, collegial, safe relationship in the work place where "the game is played."

6) The rich resources of university faculties should be consultive and hands-on to the classroom teachers, not necessarily involved in the delivery of courses. There are some outstanding educators at universities who are forced to deliver in their least attribute area teaching. Only sound models of sound practices should face teachers in groups.

7) We should temporarily deregulate accrediting agencies. Their rules prevent results, wasting effort, money, and focus.

8) There should be professional schools, locally based, that receive 100% of the FTEs. Faculties should report to district schools — being independent, yet acting as partners in causing student growth.

9) The governance of all teacher education should be the best educators both from the client group and from the industry. Industry educators are decades ahead in training personnel how to succeed and gain corporate results.

How do we get from here to there? By putting job security aside and assuming that capable contributors to the enterprise will land on their feet. We should do it because we are currently wasting billions in taxpayers' monies, because we have a responsibility to produce results, and because a competent teacher can be built as a champion.

In Summary

• Past school boards offered an incentive, the teachers took the incentive, the universities took two-thirds of the tuition money and used it for other programs.

• The incentive didn't produce a better teacher, and the universities declared teaching as an "academic pursuit."

• Now is the time for the profession and society to declare where the money will flow, and for what purpose. School boards and collective bargaining units must clarify where the next generation of incentives should be. Teacher educators must have incentives, both intrinsic and extrinsic, beyond the K-12 salary guide.

> The only thing that's going to turn the schools around is to start turning the decision making as to what works and what doesn't work over to the people who are actually doing the work and know what's happening in classrooms.[30]

We need to make changes in the way in which teachers are trained. Now is the ideal time to implement such changes, regardless of who the sponsors may be. Change will be least disruptive as the profession replaces itself.

I believe and state in this book what David Cohen says in his study "Teaching Practice from a Practitioner's Perspective" that:

Our aim in what follows, then, is to consider teaching from the teachers' perspective. This does not mean relying only on teachers' ideas about their work, nor does it mean ignoring academic analysis of teaching. It means, rather, that we consider teaching from the perspective of the work that practitioners do. What sort of work is it? What sort of problems must teachers regularly solve? What must they know and do to turn in a good performance? How do they learn?...Such questions about teaching and learning perhaps cannot be answered well until we have a reasonable idea of the teacher's trade.[31]

Teachers must not only know the subject matter for their chosen field, they must learn the skills necessary to communicate their expertise in their field to an audience of students.

Further I believe that the profession is savvy and sophisticated. The profession has a pool of highly competent, committed educators who, when asked the right questions in the right manner, will respond in the long-term interest of society and the profession.

We are at a five-year window of time, where the vast majority of teachers and teacher educators are retiring. The profession and society have a window of opportunity to correct serious errors of past judgment at a time when implementation would hurt the smallest number of people.

It's clear how we got to this point in the history of teacher education. What we must make equally clear is our determination not to be ruled by the past. We must stop stringing telegraph wires from wooden poles in an era when thousands of words per second flash from earth stations to satellites and back to another part of the globe.

We must recognize the times in which we live, and take charge of them.

Chapter 3

Where Will We Find the Money?

"This will never be a civilized country until we expend more money for books than we do for chewing gum." —
Elbert Hubbard

H arry S. Truman's famous phrase, "the buck stops here," is much more than a figure of speech. Realistically, state and provincial school districts will inherit the responsibility for funding the teacher reform movement. The buck will stop there.

The Carnegie Report, looking at what will be expected of teachers in the coming century, addressed the costs of education reform:

> This reform will be expensive. But we are convinced it is affordable. Indeed, if the investment is made over a 10-year period, we need only ensure that our public schools receive no less a share of the Gross National Product than they now enjoy. Even if the nation fails to make this investment, the cost of education will still rise, but the national resources to pay for it will suffer as America becomes increasingly noncompetitive in world markets."[32]

Revenue Sources Do Exist

We must remember that intangible revenue sources exist which can contribute to district coffers. For example, the salary differential between retiring veteran teachers' pay and novice teacher salaries will assume increased importance as those at the top of the salary guide retire and are replaced by less expensive beginning teachers.

There is, of course, great variability nationwide in the dollars and cents figures we are discussing. When top-of-the-scale teachers in New York retire at $46,000 and those in Mississippi may finish their careers at $24,000, it is true that amounts saved by the retirement of experienced faculty and the influx of new teachers will vary, state by state.

If the retiring salary of a teacher is $36,000 and the beginning salary is $18,000 and 30 teachers are retiring, that represents a money pool of $540,000 a year.

It is a worthwhile exercise to explore what the "graying" of America's teacher force means, in dollars and cents, to *your* district.

Another incalculable amount can be saved by decreasing vandalism and absenteeism in the schools. Vandalism for one suburban New Jersey high school district with which I am familiar ran more than $150,000 per year against a $3 million budget.

This is a substantial amount of money — money that could be saved by improving the overall school climate. The fact is, schools with positive climates have less destruction. By training teachers to be more positive and more effective, districts may be able to save substantial amounts of training money out of this "frustration overhead."

Absenteeism is a double-edged sword that costs money whether the individual who is absent is a student or a teacher.

States reimburse local school districts on a per diem basis for student attendance. If the student is absent, the reimbursement amount per pupil per day is lost to the district. If the student actually drops out of school at age 16, when he or she is eligible to attend two additional years, the district has lost $4,000 to $6,000 in each of those two years for just that one student dropout alone.

Teacher absenteeism costs a district money, as well. Districts must bear the expense for substitute teachers and also pay the regular classroom teacher for a certain number of contractually negotiated "sick days." A district must ask itself, when the "sick days" become excessive, whether the teachers in that district are displaying symptoms of fatigue and burnout. If that is the case, the district may reclaim much of this lost time and money by making teachers more effective, and their lives less stressful.

The most important savings will occur when all teachers are trained so competently that every minute in front of a class is a productive minute. Training of generic teaching skills produces teacher cost- effectiveness.

So, to recap, the district has a potential pool of money available for reforms in teacher education that will come from the difference between the higher salaries of retiring teachers and the lower starting salaries of beginning teachers. In addition, effective teacher training can help plug the leaks that are draining district funds — leaks like vandalism, teacher and student absenteeism.

The Private Sector Knows

A survey of one of the top business training programs in the United States, the NCR training program located in Dayton, Ohio, attempted to identify practices that could help teacher developers improve inservice training in the public schools. Over 112,000 persons were enrolled in some 650 NCR courses taught by about 800 full-time and part-time instructors.[33] NCR has 65,000 employees and customers in 120 countries around the world and develops over 100 new products yearly.[34]

Chairman W.S. Anderson of the NCR Board articulated NCR's corporate policy this way:

"The costs of identifying individuals with exceptional potential and preparing them to assume large responsibilities through development of this potential are considered as much an investment in the future as funds invested in new product development....We're devoting a great deal of time and money to the strengthening of our human resources to meet these challenges, and we expect this investment to yield a very good return."[35]

Fred H. Wood, who surveyed the NCR training, observed: "If the materials, courses, or programs needed for NCR personnel are already available in the market, they are purchased and adapted or adopted. The source of the original development is secondary to whether what is being considered for purchase adequately supports the objectives the teacher developer wishes to achieve. If it does, and costs less to purchase than to develop at NCR, it is purchased."[36]

Thus, it follows that purchasing already established and field-tested teacher development programs for schools is cost efficient.

Mr. Wood further stated that, "Superintendents and boards of education must place a high priority on teacher development for teachers and administrators. This priority needs to be stated publicly as part of district policy and be accompanied by the allocation or re-allocation of resources to provide the staff, money, and time to ensure that adequate personnel development programs are planned and implemented."[37]

"Staff development programs," noted Mr. Wood, "enable the existing and new personnel to improve their performance to carry out new roles and responsibilities."[38]

Get Your Money's Worth

Speaking of educational results, Henry M. Levin says in Cost-Effectiveness: A Primer: "It is important to emphasize that both the cost and effectiveness aspects are important and must be integrated." [39]

The secret of good teacher development is to deliver.

A district invests $20,000 to $30,000 in *teacher* costs simply by committing its 20 teachers to a week of instruction. That figure represents salary plus benefits.

Instruction costs are in addition to that. Instructor cost for one week's instruction for the group would be $3,000. Materials would cost approximately another $1,500 and courtesies $1,000, for a total cost to the district of $35,500. (Training expense estimates are based on the cost of typical training by Performance Learning Systems or a comparable training organization.)

That $35,500 seems like a whopper. It is actually a reasonable cost.

If those 20 teachers each learn 25 skills during their week's training — skills over which the teachers have demonstrated mastery — that's a grand total of 500 skill and performance patterns the district has obtained for its staff.

Our total cost figure of $35,500, divided by the 500 skills mastered, equals $71 per internalized skill. A skill that will enhance a teaching career for a lifetime...that's a bargain!

There's more! If you put teachers in class for lectures and have them spend evenings writing papers, and none of the activity has anything to do with how they are able to manage their classes to produce better student learning, and *no one* changes or acquires practical skills, the cost per result is $35,000 for *nothing*.

The expense of training must be viewed as cost per result.

Cost based on results is a measurement that has never been applied to teacher training. It should be. The tax-paying public rightfully expects teachers to be properly skilled to fulfill the learning needs of all students.

The cost of educating one student for a year, on the U.S. national average, is $4,263.[40] When a teacher faces 25 students the district cost per day is close to $600...well over $100 an hour! It costs more than $106,000 a year to have those 25 students in class. If a teacher is 20% less effective than he or she can be, a lot of the district's teaching money is wasted.

Money spent to train teachers to be more effective in the classroom is money saved.

Teacher educators in colleges and universities need to ask and to answer the same questions that private sector trainers (and executives) have been asking and answering for the past two decades. The questions the colleges and universities need to ask are:

1) What value are we getting for dollars spent?
2) What benefits can we be assured of receiving as a result of the training?
3) How will we know that the performance improvement exists?

An untrained teacher in the classroom has a variety of costs. Those costs are the district dollars that are being wasted when the teacher in front of students in the classroom is doing a poor job, or when that teacher is failing to live up to his or her full classroom potential. This dollars and cents loss to the district can be substantial. Teachers' abilities to communicate clearly to students, to motivate them, to handle critical incidents, and to deliver curriculum through specialized learning channels, are vital to a district's financial health.

The reform movement is upon us. Positive signs show that the funding necessary for implementing much needed improvement in teacher education is being found. It is up to the educational establishment to take these dollars, and, following industry's lead, make a dynamic difference.

Ongoing teacher training to ensure cost efficient education can be a reality. The future cost to society for failing to act now will be infinitely more expensive than doing the right thing today.

The buck has stopped here, right in front of us.

Chapter 4 **Observing the Performance**

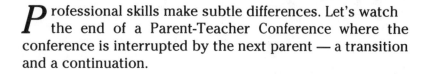

"Simplicity is synonymous with elegance but don't confuse simple with being easy"—Virginia Satire

*P*rofessional skills make subtle differences. Let's watch the end of a Parent-Teacher Conference where the conference is interrupted by the next parent — a transition and a continuation.

1. Woman: Oh, excuse me.

2. Teacher: I'll be with you in a few minutes. Would you wait outside please?

3. Woman: I didn't mean to intrude.

4. Teacher: Uh, where were we?

5. Mother: We were talking about John's science experiment.

6. Teacher: Well, John is careful and deliberate, though he's awfully slow in getting the job done.

7. Teacher: Is he that way at home too?

8. Mother: Well, yes. He hates to make a mistake.

The trained observer will often note that somehow the total impact of the teacher is negative. Others will suggest it was OK. Let's look at this frame by frame.

1. Woman: Oh, excuse me.

Because the teacher is seated at the front of the room, with his back to the door, it is necessary for the incoming parent to interrupt the conference. It would be better to hold the conference at the back of the room, away from the door (unless the door is at the back of the room, in which case the set-up would be reversed). That would enable the teacher to silently greet incoming parents. (Skill of Tactical Emplacement)

2. Teacher: I'll be with you in a minute.
Would you wait outside please?

Because many parents approach conferences with a certain amount of anxiety, instead of asking the parent to wait outside, the teacher might have invited the parent in to take a seat and to look over her child's folder (which would have been set out beforehand). If coffee had been set up at the front of the room by the parents' group, there could be relatively easy transitions between conferences. Such a reception area would make the entering parent more comfortable than having to wait in the hall and would avoid the possibility of the seated parent's feeling she was taking up too much time. (Skills of Group Dynamics and the VIP Game)

3. Woman: I didn't mean to intrude.

As she said, she felt she was intruding on the conference. Again, had there been a different set-up for the conference, with parents entering at the front while the conference went on in the back, there would have been no feeling of interruption. The parent would simply come in and sit down to look at her child's folder and have a cup of coffee while waiting.

4. Teacher: Uh, where were we?

The teacher's "Where were we?" might be construed by the parent as evidence of his not being heavily enough involved in their conversation to remember what they were talking about. As soon as he was interrupted by the incoming parent, he should have made a mental note of what they had been discussing. (Skill of Handling Transitions)

5. Mother: We were talking about John's science experiment.

Covering his mouth with his hand while the parent brought him up-to-date might imply that he was holding something back — perhaps a yawn — signaling lack of interest — or an unconscious wish to say something indiscreet. His lack of eye contact with the parent also indicates lack of interest, as does his posture of leaning somewhat away from, instead of toward, the parent. It would have been far better to have leaned interestedly toward the parent and made direct, involved eye contact, openly showing involvement by not covering his mouth. (Skills of five point stance, eye contact, and open body language)

6. Teacher: Well, John is careful and deliberate, though he's awfully slow in getting the job done.

The teacher's apparent approval statement — that John is careful and deliberate — was a left-handed one, counteracted by the characterization of the boy as "awfully slow to get the job done." What the parent heard most loudly was the criticism, not the approval. The teacher would better have said, "John is very careful and deliberate in his work. He takes a great deal of time to get the job done."

In addition, he seems, while he is talking, to be preoccupied with his grade book; the parent might conclude that he is more interested in grades than in the student's work or the student as an individual. Referring to the student's work folder instead would have created a better climate between him and the parent. (Skills of five-point stance, eye contact, and open body language)

7. Teacher: Is he that way at home too?

Leaning in toward the parent now may be perceived as an aggressive move, arousing the parent's defenses, as might the teacher's meeting the parent's eyes deliberately, after having avoided them before. The closed-ended question assumes the parent agrees. An open-ended question would be better. For example, "What do you notice at home?" (Counseling skill, Skill of body language)

8. Mother: Well, yes. He hates to make a mistake.

As predicted, the parent perceived the teacher as aggressive and thus retreated way back into her chair in defense.

> When we first viewed this conference, it *seemed* pretty much all right. There may have been a nagging feeling that there was *something* wrong. We were picking up uncomfortable vibrations, double messages.

> Putting the interview in perspective, it's unlikely that the parent came away feeling she had had a *poor* conference — just the same kind of undefined, vague feelings we had that something was amiss.

> Advertising research says that 78% of the message is visual, 13% of the message is tonal, and 9% of the message is the word structures. While percentages may be different to teaching or parent conferences, what the client sees and hears in tone is often the greater message. The teacher above might be the best teacher in the school. Unfortunately, subtle performance differences in this less than one-minute conference had to negatively affect both parents.

Teaching is made up of sets of "teaching instances." A teaching instance has four stages:

1) Reading the present environment, i.e., body language and tone qualities of the students, allotted time, lesson goals, etc.,
2) Deciding what environmental cue is priority,
3) Deciding which skill will be filled with what content, and
4) Performing "live" the teaching instance.

Below are teaching instances showing the teacher performing teaching instances. The first four are well done. The last teacher shows the discrepancy between what was and what could have been. The purpose of this chapter is to connect skills to teaching instances. It's designed to show how skills (the actual performance) produce desirable and undesirable conclusions.

B J Zielinski is one of those clear and precise teachers who has little wasted motion.

Narrator: BJ Zielinski demonstrates abstract/sequential organization in her lesson on numerical dating and the 24-hour clock.

Teacher: We're going to learn two aspects of the metric system — numerical dating and the 24-hour clock. (Note how BJ closes the distance between herself and the students)

T: If you go into the armed services or pick up a travel schedule to fly anywhere in the world, the times and dates are metric.
    (The Compelling Why Skill — Note how BJ uses her fingers to sequentially complement her Compelling Why)

T: I understand that many job applications require metric dating.
>   (Compelling Why Skill)

T: Be confident that, once you understand it, you'll find it easy.
>   (Positive Phrasing Skill)
>   [End of a Teaching Instance]

T: Let's have a look at numerical dating first.
>   (Sequencing Skill)

T: We'll take today's date as an example.
>   (An Instance Skill)

T: It's as simple as . . . 1982 . . . 04 for April, the 4th month . . . 02 for the second day.
>   (Sequential Skill. Note how she underlines pertinent information on the board)

T: It goes from the largest time, the year, to the smallest time, the day.
>   (Provides the generalization clearly)

T: That's all, the whole story.
>   (Positive Phrasing Skill)
>   [End of a Teaching Instance]

T: I bet you thought there was more. Let's apply it to *your* birthdays.
   (A Memory Hook Skill)

N: All the students write their birthdays in numerical dating, and BJ collects some representative samples.
   [End of a Teaching Instance]

T: The 24-hour clock is convenient because it avoids a.m. and p.m. First, you move around the a.m., in blue.
   (Color Coding Skill, Sequencing)

T: And then around the p.m., in red. It's that simple.
   [End of a Teaching Instance]

After a thorough explanation and practice of the 24-hour clock, BJ handed out travel folders from Club Med. Each student became a travel agent. She reviewed the document. She called up on the telephone, acting the role of a client, and asked questions of the travel agent (student). The student responded to her enquiries. What you can't see is her extraordinary skills of timing, pace, and acting ability. She was totally believable as different "clients." The students role-played as competent travel agents with a warm-up, client-need questions, and technical competence as to arrivals and departures converting a.m. and p.m. times to the 24-hour clock.

Charlie Young has used several selected pictures of the Midwest. He had students see pictures (images) where they interpreted the visual. He is trying to develop foreground-background visual discrimination skills with his students.

T: Look carefully at the picture. What do you suppose this is . . . (10-second pause) . . . Randy?
>   (Charlie gives students plenty of time to evaluate the picture — clarity of question)

S: It's something to hold animals.

T: Good. Why do you think so?
>   (Evaluation Probe Skill)

S: Well, I can see slats and what look like pens.

T: How large would you say it is?
>   (Comprehension Probe Skill)

S: It's very big. There are probably parts that can't be seen in the picture. It probably holds cattle.

T: Thumbs up. It's the Chicago stockyards, where the cattle are auctioned for the meat packing houses.
   (Approval and Deductive Statement)
   [End of a Teaching Instance]

T: I showed those two pictures because they are two images that remind me of the Midwest. Farms and factories. We will get to know all kinds of businesses related to farming and meat packing.
   (Visual Hook Memory Skill)

N: The class continues with a discussion of the business and services related to farming and meat packing.
   (A set of instances — Discussion is kinesthetic and auditory, thus completing a Kinesthetic/Tactual Auditory/Visual rotation)

T: Let's return to our gameboard map. Over the next two weeks you'll have the opportunity to move your company ahead, to show a profit or a loss.
   (Compelling Why Skill)

Charlie leads up to a two-week simulation "businessman's game" that allows students to make profits and take losses in trading commodities, manufactured products, and services of the Midwest. The intensity and involvement of students was extraordinary. Simulations are powerful teachers even though they don't follow a 7-step lesson plan.

Dale Hodorek is presenting an inductive lesson. Her goal is to process examples of words that "sound the same, yet have different spellings and meanings" (homonyms). She uses an inductive process.

N: Dale Hodorek's sense of humor is reflected in her classroom.

N: We join her at the beginning of a language arts lesson.

T: I'm going to show you some pictures and say a sentence about each one. In each sentence you will hear two words that sound the same. See if you can find out what they are. Listen for them.
  (Skill of Clarity)

T: Before dark, this family *would* gather *wood* for the campfire.
  (Skill of using a visual)

T: Which words sound the same . . . (3-second pause) . . . Janice?
  (Skill of Clarity
  Skill of Pause Time)

S: Wood?
  [End of a Teaching Instance]

T: Righto. Now the next one. The *pain* in Joan's hand came from the cut she got on the broken window *pane*.
  (Skill of Approval
  Skill of Clarity
  Skill of distinctiveness of each word
  Skill of upstaging the environment
  Skill of using a visual)

T: Mary?

S: Pain.
  [End of Teaching Instance]

T: We're really rolling now. How about this one: Mother will *wait* while Jimmy chooses the cheese with the correct *weight.*
  (Skill of Approval
  Skill of Clarity
  Skill of distinctiveness of each word
  Skill of upstaging the environment
  Skill of using a visual)

T: Jesse?

S: Wait?
  [End of Teaching Instance]

T: We've got the hang of it now. Now, this one . . .
  (Skill of Approval
  Skill of Clarity
  Skill of distinctiveness of each word
  Skill of upstaging the environment
  Skill of using a visual)

T: Now, let's take a look at these lists I have on the board. The blue list has words that sound like the words on the green list. Who wants to come up and draw a line between two words that sound alike? How about you . . . (5-second pause) . . . Bobby?
  (Skill of color coding lists
  Skill of Clarity
  Skill of Pause Time)
  [End of Teaching Instance]

T: Ate and eight. Terrific, Bobby. How about you . . . Jeremy?
  (Skill of Approval
  Skill of Clarity
  Skill of distinctiveness of each word
  Skill of upstaging the environment
  Skill of using a visual)

T: Bee and be. Excellent match.
    (Skill of Approval
    Skill of Clarity
    Skill of distinctiveness of each word
    Skill of upstaging the environment
    Skill of using a visual)

T: How about a big hand for Bobby and Jeremy?
    (Positive Body Language
    Upstaging the environment)
    [End of Teaching Instance]

Kids applaud.
    (Skill of reward
    Skill of expending physical energy in group
    celebration)
    [End of Teaching Instance]

T: Harold, you have a match?

T: I bet it's a good one.
    (Skill of reward)

T: Oh, that is good. Harold matched deer and dear. Next.
    (Skill of reward)

T: We'll have just a few more before we go on . . . Mary?

T: Clever, Mary. How about you . . . Melissa?
    (Skill of approval)

T: Fine. What two words did Melissa join together . . .

T: Debbie?

S: Right and write.

T: Good!
    (Skill of reward)

T: Now, these words sound the same. How are these words
    different? . . . (5-second pause) . . . Andre?
        (Skill of pause time
         Skills of SDLOC: Same, Different,
         Label, Operate, Combine)

S: They're spelled differently and have different meanings.
        (Dale allowed the students to make a generalization
         through a succession of instances — the inductive
         process)

T: That was a toughie. Let's give Andre a big hand.
        (Skill of Approval
         Skill of celebration)

T: They are called homonyms. Say it aloud and imagine the
    meaning — now.

S: HOM - O - NYMS

T: Again.

S: HOM - O - NYMS
    (Notice how Dale employs their generalization to
    the term and gets every student to say the word
    aloud several times by imaging)

The lesson continues. Dale finishes her lesson with this
memory hook skill — a rhyme the students recite together:
"Homonyms can fool you because they sound the same, but
how they look and what they mean can trick you in the game."
(Auditory Memory Hook)

Jim East does a synthesis exercise to improve creativity
in writing. Before beginning this exercise, the students cleared
an area in the classroom by stacking every desk and every
chair against the walls — quietly and in two minutes. This
exercise and others that he employs are highly active
(kinesthetic-tactual).

T: Now we're going to march, clockwise and counter-
    clockwise, and in "S" shapes.

T: Remember, the trick is never to touch anyone else.

T: When I give you three words, stop and talk to the person nearest you about that subject.

T: I'll turn on the music.

T: And you start marching.
     (Notice his directions are clear and concise)

T: Field, police officer, abandoned car.
     (Notice he is participating in the marching too — a positive nonverbal)

S: An old man, I'm not sure where he came from, was living in an *abandoned car* in a *field* near some trees. The neighbors complained to the *police*.
     [End of Teaching Instance]

T: Crowded restaurant, celebrity, hail storm.

S: It was *hailing* outside. It sounded like thunder on the roof. But the *restaurant* was *crowded* because *Margaret Thatcher* was *holding* a *press conference*.
     [End of Teaching Instance]

The exercise took 20 minutes in the middle of the period plus 4 minutes in stacking and unstacking desks and chairs. Note that every student gave a sentence during every march, which, as a package, was a student synthesis statement every 2 minutes. Jim executed skills of clarity, directions, enthusiasm in voice, nonverbal and tone qualities that upstaged the environment. What can't be seen in the pictures is how intensely he listens to students with sympathetic eye movements and speaks up (versus down) to students. That type of modeling causes students to talk and work respectfully with each other.

Let's look at another teacher:

1. Sounds of kids talking.

2. Bell rings.

3. Girls chattering.

4. Girls, the bell has rung. Take out your books.

5. Sounds of papers rustling.

The teacher could have begun the day more enthusiastically and with greater involvement with her students. Rather than sitting behind her desk, which is a barrier, she might have been standing at the door while the students filed in. When the bell rang, she could have stood immediately in front of her desk, smiled, and used the skills of eye contact, name dropping, and moving in with the girls. If she had, the Authority Statement may not have been necessary.

Her Authority Statement to the two girls who continued to talk after the bell was appropriate; her facial expression was only mildly annoyed. The teacher succeeded in bringing the girls to attention.

Later in the class period . . .

Sounds of laughter from class as student comes in late.
　　(Time for a nonconfrontation strategy)

T: Rich, you're late again.
　　(Confirmatory paraphrase — Note negative body language.)

T: You know you're expected to be here on time.
　　(Positive phrasing skill — Note double message between body language, tone of voice, and words. Also, she should be facing almost all students most of the time. Yet here she has her back to most students.)

S: I told ya. I can't always get here on time from shop.

S: Yeah, we can't always get here on time. With the new addition they're putting on, we can hardly move in the halls.
　　(Note the group dynamics of the boy defending the late student and the late student's smug look. We strongly recommend writing the student's name down, and handling the late student one-on-one at a transition point during the class period.)

T: I know it's difficult. Just do the best you can.
   (Empathy Statement skill — Note body language
   and tonality is hostile which makes the empathy
   appear dishonest.)

T: OK. Yesterday we were discussing bacteria. Tami, tell me,
   if you remember, what bacteria need to thrive.
   [Memory level question skill. The question has too
   many words. It should have been asked: "What
   does bacteria need to thrive . . . (3-second pause)
   . . . Tami?"
   ". . . tell me, if you remember" is unnecessary. The
   teacher should have begun with a Compelling
   Why.]

S: Uh, water, food, light, uh . . .

S: Uh, oxygen, uh . . .

T: Would you correct Tami's error, Howard?
   [This is a negatively stated probe.
     Perhaps a closed ended question would be more
     appropriate, such as: "Does all bacteria need
     oxygen?" or "You are right about food and light"
     (Approval Statement).
     "Think about oxygen" (probe).
     Note that crossed arms are often associated with
     disapproval.]

S: What error?

T: Don't you know what's wrong with Tami's answer? She said *all* bacteria need oxygen.

> (Again, the teacher's negative tone provides negative fear in Howard. The positive approval for 3 of 4 correct answers, with a quizzical question about oxygen would have avoided Howard's negative feelings.)

Certainly the teacher should have responded to Tami's answer using one of the techniques covered in the Art of Questioning. She could still have used Student Accountability with Howard, without arousing hostility: "Which part of Tami's answer is correct . . . (3-second pause) . . . Howard?"

T: Karla, do *all* bacteria need oxygen?

S: Karla, she called on you.

S: Would you repeat the question please?

T: The question was, do *all* bacteria need oxygen? Do they? And if they don't all need oxygen, what kinds do and what kinds don't?

> (Note the teacher's confrontation stance. The memory level question based on yesterday's lesson has too many words. The question should have been: "Do all bacteria need oxygen?" — eliminating the other two questions.)

This teacher, in the context of her whole persona, is highly trainable and coachable. She loves her subject and does want to do a good job. She is inadvertently so focused on her lesson that she needs to read her own tonal qualities/body language as being the cause of the students' body language. She needs to internalize the reading of nonverbal signals, her own and the students' (12 hours of training), of classroom questions (20 hours of training), nonconfrontational and momentum strategies (6 hours of training), and Compelling Why (3 hours of training). The above scenario demonstrates how a teacher can produce a negative spiral. As Pogo said, "We have met the enemy and he is us."

If I were her coach, without training, I would have her use alternative skills for instant success:

• Open class with love and enthusiasm
• Follow with a Compelling Why
• Get the teacher in the habit of noting the names of latecomers and waiting for a transition period to say something to them
• Get the teacher to frame questions with as few words as possible

When we compare the first four teachers with the last teacher, we see within each "teaching instance" that the first four have students on-task and the last teacher is causing the off-task behaviors she wants to avoid.

The differences are the mental processes and performances. Teachers have to learn and trust that various centers of their brains can process reading the environment simultaneously. Teachers have to trust that while they are delivering a skill/content package — they can simultaneously read the audience to gain a cue as to where to go next. In a fraction of a second or several seconds, the teacher sorts skill and content options — automatically, the teacher makes a "will do" decision and executes the next performance. It's the process of analysis and then physical synthesis.

For training purposes, we think through the teacher's eyes as to what stimuli to pay attention to when (cues vs. noise), then what skill options will solve the cue of the teaching instance, then follow with the performance which would be the word structure, tonality, and body language.

All people, including teachers, process similar instances together. The natural process of the mind is to allow similar instances or experiences to form together. Therefore, similar, or like, instance categories can be formed for handling correct answers, the late student, the inductive process, the kicking foot, the smart remark, the lesson opener, the Compelling Why, etc. All people, including teachers, learn fastest/longer by applying generic skills to generic teaching instances. Internalization occurs when the teacher gets a cue, acts on the cue, and it works.

Smoothness and "with-it-ness" alluded to in the research are the teacher's ability to correctly read, decide, and perform. PLS has had tremendous success with training generic skills to generic teaching events and gaining transfer. We can say generally (with some exceptions) that smoothness and with-it-ness are trainable, as are teaching skills and decision patterns. The degree to which sound practice is trainable often depends on the natural abilities of teachers to read events, gain the most relevant cue, access the skill choices, and sense how the performance came across. This parallels predispositions to being musical or athletic where the combination of natural predisposition and training is the catalyst to greatness.

Championship teachers learn skills by being trained in specific situations, events they will encounter in teaching. Under the eye of expert coaches, champions are developed.

Chapter 5

Teaching Is a Performing Art

"Each honest calling, each walk of life, has its own elite, its own aristocracy, based on excellence of performance."—James Bryant Conant

*T*he actor and the teacher have a great deal in common. Teaching is a performing art comparable to acting, playing music, and Olympic skating or diving. It requires precision and finesse in the execution of highly honed skills.

Konstantin Stanislavski, the great Russian theoretician and originator of the Stanislavski Method of acting, preached that ". . .an actor has to learn anew to see and not just to pretend to see, to hear and not just to pretend to listen, that he has to talk to his fellow actors and not just to read lines, that he has to think and feel."[41] Insert the word "teacher" for "actor" in that quote, and you have statements that apply equally well to teaching as a performing art.

What set Orson Welles, Bette Davis, Richard Burton, and Liv Ullman apart from other amateur and professional actors? The high level of precision and finesse of fundamental skills they called upon to communicate successfully and efficiently under conditions of stress, made the difference. Acting and teaching are, indeed, both performing arts; both are situations where the skills of the trade must constantly be adapted for new situations.

The Right Approach Is Effective

N.L. Gage wrote, in "What Do We Know About Teaching Effectiveness?":

> Teaching is an instrumental or practical art, not a fine art. As an instrumental art, teaching departs from recipes, formulas, and algorithms. It requires improvisation, spontaneity, the handling of a vast array of considerations of form, style, pace, rhythm, and appropriateness in ways so complex that even

computers must lose the way, just as they cannot achieve what a mother does with a five year old.[42]

Teaching is different from some of the other performing arts because the teacher does not face a totally predictable situation each classroom day. In teaching, you never know what the dynamics of that day's classes might be.

Who can predict, in advance, that Jane will start art class by shoving clay up Harvey's nose, necessitating an emergency trip to the nurse? Can you know beforehand that Alfredo will be upset over his parents' impending divorce, that Betsy's rabbit just died, or that Sandy told Bob right before your class that she "wouldn't go to the dance with him if he were the last boy on the planet"?

Teaching is mostly free-form, even if there is a lesson plan for that day's class. Sometimes experience dictates leaving the plan because of the teacher's "reading" of the students. This is not surprising in an environment where over 1,500 interactions per day take place with different students on different issues — all while the teacher is simultaneously supervising classes of about thirty students.

Robert McNergney and Lyn Satterstrom wrote in "Teacher Characteristics and Teacher Performance":

> Whether they know it or not, teachers are involved in improvisational activities all the time....Lessons may be carefully planned over both the short and long haul, yet almost daily adjustments are necessary as students and teachers interact in a dizzying dynamic that requires the utmost in spontaneity and imagination.[43]

The similarity between teaching and other performing arts is that teachers are in sympathetic interaction with their students. There is an ebb and flow between them.

In fact, research confirms that outstanding teachers are attracted to a profession that offers independence and an opportunity to be creative.

Louis Rubin in an article entitled "The Artist Teacher" compared gifted teaching to artistry in fields such as music.[44] The teacher and the jazz musician must both use a variety of proficiencies with precision and finesse in order to succeed. The premier jazz musician, playing ensemble, combines technical skill with emotional meaning, playing off the group and the audience to produce an elegant sound. Teaching as a performing art can be experienced best from the perspective of elegant teachers, from the way they hear, see, move, and feel. As one teacher said:

> I love teaching because it uses all of me — my hands, my body, my face, my eyes, and my voice, including inflection, pause, and volume. I have to use my heart and my mind to process everything around me and understand what it all means. Then I can organize myself to lead my students toward hope, confidence, knowledge, comprehension, creativity, judgment, common sense, and group sense. All the time that I am teaching, I am processing many complexities in my mind. I'm like a jazz group, always aware that all the parts mesh with the whole. It's complex and challenging — and I love it!

Larry Cuban reminds us that teaching is closer to carving marble than to making cars, that "first rate teaching is personal, closer to an art than a science,"[45] and that "schooling is not an assembly line where teachers produce a predictable flow of well-behaved children, chock full of facts and sporting ever higher test scores."[46]

Teaching cannot be taught in the same ways that we train assembly line workers, aircraft mechanics, or medical technicians.

A Stream of Decisions

Madeline Hunter tells us that, "Teaching can be defined as a constant stream of decisions made before, during and after interaction with the learner: decisions which, when implemented, increase the probability of learning. Teacher development which promotes an increasingly sophisticated basis for making those decisions is an essential continuing aspect of effective schooling."[47]

David K. Cohen in his study, "Teaching Practices from the Practitioner's Perspective," commented on this same improvisational nature of teaching, saying:

> Improvisation often requires quick decisions, and on-the-spot adjustments of existing skills to novel circumstances. In this sense most practitioners learn as they work, devising somewhat novel procedures or inventing slightly different goals, adjusting what they know to what they couldn't predict. In extending their experience they broaden their competence. [48]

Like actors, teachers should be — must be — trained in vocal tonality, modulation, pitch, timbre, and volume, the fundamentals of verbal performance. In addition, the successful actor on stage exercises superb control over his or her physical presence. Each eye movement, facial expression, hand gesture, and body movement communicates meaning with impact, integrated fully with the vocal projection.[49]

As a performing art, teaching is highly definable. It can be trained, modeled, coached, internalized, documented, and evaluated.

While teaching skills are primarily simple and definable, the complexity of elegant teaching arises in the act of combining simple skills in a sequence or using several skills at the same time. This ability, **multiple concentration**, is the cornerstone of elegant teaching, and will be covered in detail in a later chapter.

There should be a vast difference between the training of a historian, an accountant, or an engineer — who crafts sequential, single-focus mental activities — and a teacher who has to sort meaning out of stimuli and simultaneously execute a performance.

Predisposition toward multiple concentration parallels predispositions toward mathematics, music, or art. The greater the predisposition, the higher the level of sophistication that can be achieved. The superstars in the performing arts began with very strong predispositions toward their fields.[50]

It appears that professional performing artists as a group possess two critical skills: the ability to read situations and the ability to simultaneously execute a performance.

Consider another performing artist, the professional football quarterback. The best of quarterbacks, like the best of all performing artists, trains constantly to develop and internalize the fundamental skills to the highest possible level of reflexive precision and finesse. Chalk talks, films and videos of past performances, and most importantly, ongoing training and coaching on the playing field lead directly to success. The quarterback assesses what's happening in the game, notes strengths and weaknesses, calculates plays that should work, reads the defense, judges one play against another, makes a choice of strategies, and executes the chosen strategy.

Like the football quarterback, the teacher also has a playbook of skills, proficiencies, and strategies. The teacher conducting a class has a game plan, a set of plays, and players upon whose attributes she or he can capitalize. Leading with optimism, he or she projects a "can do" attitude, which is referred to in much of the literature as a "sense of efficacy."

Occasionally, strategies have to be changed on the line of scrimmage in response to changing conditions. Cohen also noted this about teachers when he said, "The skills of teaching are not a fixed stock, they cannot be learned once and for all. In a sense, they must be learned over and over as they are adapted to particular interactions."[51]

Advanced, exquisite teaching requires the use of these proficiencies, just as the acting profession adds subtleties such as hands and vocal pitch up for visual verbs, hands and vocal pitch down for kinesthetic/tactual verbs, and hands and vocal pitch in mid-range for auditory verbs. For the actor and the teacher, voice and body language are synchronized with the color, brilliance, and texture of the words in the message.

Teachers and negotiators share the art of persuasion and use of power. Teachers and lawyers share the skill of organizing a case into learnable units and then employing a question and explanation strategy for their presentation. A teacher's "case" is to persuade the "jury" of students that learning what is being taught is desirable.

Teachers and physicians diagnose and prescribe. When the student appears perplexed and communicates, "I still don't understand," the teacher has to diagnose the problem and execute a new prescription. Learning problems vary greatly and the teacher has to have a huge pharmacopoeia of cures a synapse snap away.

Teachers and detectives share the intuitive ability to read people and events. Teachers have to judge the "truthfulness" of situations, gather testimony, gauge silence, evaluate inconsistencies, build composites, and make judgments. Students judge teacher "fairness" high on their priority list. Both teachers and detectives collect many bits of evidence and data and process them to synthesize a course of action.

Whether individually or in groups, teachers are outnumbered twenty or forty to one. Therefore, teachers have to be persuasive to achieve the group mission. They often have to persuade by making judicious power judgments. Teachers are constantly making complex judgments as to whether to keep, share, and/or give up power to students in the context of a highly structured school setting. At times, teachers must negotiate with peers, parents, or administrators. All of these shared mental processes consist of closure, prescription, and execution.

Hidden Messages

Research verifies that vocal tonality and body language can profoundly affect the messages our words convey, even to the point of communicating unintended or covert signals.[52] When a teacher crosses the arms, leans back, shakes the head with a frown and knitted eyebrows, and says, "What are you doing?" with an emphasis on the words "what" and "you," the meaning of the message is apparently, "Stop what you are doing!" In contrast, if the teacher uses the same words with open body language, warm facial expression and eyes, and a curious tone, the message would be interpreted as "I'm curious about your activity." To deliver the message intended, a teacher's tonality and body language must be congruent with the words. Then the performance will succeed.

A typical scenario illustrates this important point. A teacher notices John's quizzical looks during a lesson covering new material. The teacher finishes his sentence and responds to John's nonverbal message — "John?"

The teacher's voice is knowing and curious.

John says, "I was wondering..." Based on John's concerns, the teacher orchestrates the lesson to teach the concept to John. He changes tonal patterns to place emphasis on some words. At the same time he is gesturing with his hands and arms and using his eyes and face to communicate the importance of key words and phrases. Because the teacher has trained himself to read students' faces as well as a pro quarterback reads the opposition's defense, he is able to pick up many nonverbal signals from the students.

John's nonverbal signal said, "I'm confused," "I missed it," or "I disagree." The teacher recorded the quizzical look, completed his explanation, and then used a probe for the purpose of solving the problem.

How a teacher feels about teaching and the students is also communicated in what a teacher says, the tone of voice, and in body language, including his or her proximity to students. Teachers who dislike teaching, or have lost their enthusiasm for it, send an increasing number of mixed messages, double messages, and negative messages. For instance, the word "interesting" can be delivered in an upbeat manner, or as a put-down. I can remember my second hour

"Learning Problems" class coming in and "sizing me up." John, the irrepressible, would enter and ask Susan, "Is he in a good mood or a bad mood?"

Amused, I would interrupt, "What makes you guys think I'm in a bad mood? I told you, I'm having a good day."

"Yeah, but you've got *that* look. And your arms are folded. . ."

"Now you're fiddling with your paperweight," Lorraine would interject.

These kids were amazing! "Learning problems," my foot! These were among the most perceptive kids in the school in terms of picking up body language and incongruent messages.

As a matter of fact, this was one of my more difficult years, from a personal perspective, not from the standpoint of students. And the message was "leaking" through to the perceptive students, even when I was unaware that I was sending the signals.

To make matters worse, the students who receive these confusing messages will send back mixed, double, and negative messages of their own, continuing the teacher negative-stress spiral.

Getting Good Performances

When we view teaching as a teacher performance we will realize how a bad performance will negatively affect the audience, and just how much can be gained by training and coaching teachers in the specific skills needed to give a superior performance.

Only when we look at teaching as a performing art do we see the areas that are not covered in the educational foundations of psychology, sociology, and research. We see that teaching events are dynamic, concrete, active, and specific. While there are some distinguishable patterns to behaviors and theories, they are clearly only valuable when coupled with the highly developed, positive, reflexive skills that comprise elegant teaching.

It may be that the fundamental skills and strategies of singing, acting, dancing, poetry reading, and even playing video games are more important to the reflexive execution of elegant teaching practices than the knowledge of the foundations of sociology, psychology, statistics, and educational research. While these courses have value and are important in total teacher development, the value is secondary to training the performance of teaching.

Knowledge has a role in the development of a prima ballerina, a quarterback, an opera singer, or a surgeon, but what these people are compensated for is expert execution of skills, especially under pressure situations.

Since teachers are performing artists, current teacher education programs are out of sync with the training required in other performing arts. All performing artists train in the use of fundamental skills, working on those skills until they are reflexive.

Certainly every teacher can and should train in all the skills, and be coached until those skills can be used reflexively. Under these conditions, teachers will become performing artists truly parallel to musicians, actors, dancers, and athletes, for whom the developing and refining of fundamental skills is a lifelong pursuit.

After observing the University of South Florida's Honors Teacher Education Program which won the 1985 American Association of Colleges of Teacher Education award, we believe that their program represents an exemplary trend in teacher education. The university recruits honors students as teaching candidates by screening for the natural attributes of successful teachers, and trains them as performers. It's warmth, eye sparkle, and enthusiasm, as well as academic accomplishment, that the South Florida program seeks.

I would far prefer students possessing heightened perceptual systems and multiple concentration as teacher candidates, compared to candidates possessing only academic credentials. I challenge the researchers to demonstrate that SAT scores or academic credentials are more relevant criteria for identifying excellent teacher candidates. In a Texas A&M study it was found that a student teacher's grade point average in college coursework was a poor predictor of the student teacher's ability to bring about cognitive growth in learners.[53]

Our conclusion is that, as in the University of South Florida program, the training of teachers should be more closely patterned after the training of performing artists. There is a vast difference between appreciating music and being able to perform as a virtuoso, between being an "armchair quarterback" and being able to throw a well-executed pass.

Good Teaching Is Complex

Teaching is a complex function. It is the ability to lead, organize, synthesize, create, analyze, interpret, describe, and make decisions based on the facts. Perhaps most difficult of all is the fact that teachers must make these decisions based on incomplete facts. And even so, teaching is highly defined in skill structures and the relational hierarchies of complex thought — the skills are as defined as executing high "C." It takes years of conscientious training before opera singers can execute high "C" with precision. It takes years before a quarterback can throw a forward pass to his receivers with pinpoint accuracy. What makes elegant performing artists is the ability to execute fundamental skills in complex combinations with "pinpoint accuracy."

Pro football teams don't hire just any person who can pass a ball. Opera companies don't hire just any person who can hit high "C." They only hire those whose performance patterns are vastly superior, who can, in effect, execute with pinpoint accuracy.

Keep in mind that performing artists receive training, coaching, and then perform. They get more training, are coached, and perform again. This process continues throughout their careers. Not following this training formula has been the failing of teacher education in America. Following it can produce championship teachers.

Now is the time to discuss the merits of training teachers as performing artists and certifying them as competent professionals in the field. Now is the time to change, to begin a new day for a new generation of teachers and teacher educators.

Woven throughout the following chapters runs an underlying theme that must be inferred: If teaching is defined and can be observed, modeled, trained, coached, internalized, and documented, then the current teacher training systems and incentive systems are out of step with what we know today will produce the best teachers.

The implications of this conclusion are staggering.

Chapter 6

Characteristics of the Effective Teacher

"A teacher affects eternity; he can never tell where his influence stops."—Henry Brooks Adams

The Skills-Scenario Linkage

In the previous chapters of this book I have tried to describe a new approach to teacher education: We must start by considering teachers as performers, give them the practical skills they need to effectively perform their classroom roles, and we have to find the money to do it. Good and poor teaching can be observed in performing moves. Sound teaching can be best internalized in a skills-scenario format.

Now I'd like to take a close look at those teachers we're trying to support. Let us first recognize that we are not dealing with the same person in each case. Teachers as a group have different characteristics.

Many teachers have strengths that help them win. One teacher may excel in counseling skills. Another may ask high quality and wide-ranging classroom questions. Yet another teacher may present lessons in a very clear and concise way. Teachers with the characteristic of effective persuasion get their students enthused, develop a team spirit and a sense of group mission. Other teachers have an obvious love of the subject matter. They communicate this intense interest to their students and therefore stimulate learning.

All teachers are a combination of these characteristics. It is better to enhance a teacher's strong characteristics than to attempt to improve their weaker ones. The development of attributes can be made to happen faster than the management of liabilities. Unless we model the development of teacher attributes as teacher educators, how can we ask teachers to develop the attributes of students? If we are to respect the attributes of children, we first must respect the attributes of teachers.

Because teaching is complex, it is very hard to be a superb counsellor, a dynamic motivator, possess stimulating questioning skills, and show a passionate love of the subject matter. The wise education leader looks to see which are the strong attributes that can be made to blossom most quickly and richly.

When we give teachers classroom skill and performance patterns they will have phenomenal growth in the areas where they already are predisposed to be successful. When they become extremely successful in the areas of their existing attributes, two things will happen:

1) Their success will pull weak attributes up to a higher level.

2) Weaker attributes become less visible to students — and less important to the learning situation — when strengths are increased.

The attributes of effective teachers must be looked to during this period of reform. They are the strong foundation upon which skills training must be built. As Maria E. Defino noted, "If there can be general agreement that some teacher behaviors and methods will more than likely result in greater pupil growth than will other teacher behaviors and methods, then school districts must begin to identify those behaviors and attend closely to whether or not they are being used by teachers."[54]

Outstanding teachers exhibit natural attributes and skills. Some they are born with; some they acquire through long experience or internalize rapidly through an efficient training program. These qualities are independent of content, teaching style, grade level, or philosophy, and seem to shine forth, giving the possessor unmistakable charisma.

What are these qualities? They are warmth, leadership, positiveness, eye sparkle, upbeat tonality, believability. Great teachers possess a sparkle in the eye, a lilt in the voice, a song in their hearts, and a flair in the classroom. Whether elegant teachers are dynamic and electric or "laid back" and relaxed, they possess the following qualities, and you just can't miss 'em, even at a country mile:

1) **Positive Strokes for Little Folks:** Effective teachers use positive phrasing in negative situations. They act on the positive elements, using them to accomplish positive goals. They almost always are positive in their phrasing, employing words, tonality, and body language that are positive and upbeat.

They tell students what they want them to do, rather than what they don't want them to do. Only occasionally do they use negative phrasing, and then usually only for contrast. Ninety percent of the communication of charismatic teachers is positive. Whatever the message, effective teachers rarely send mixed messages, achieving congruent body language and tonality.

2) **Enthusiasm Is Infectious:** Effective teachers' voices communicate interest and enthusiasm. The voice almost sings and the quality is easy on the ears. Outstanding teachers are lifetime learners who communicate their excitement in discovering new knowledge to their students. Such teachers are more aware of the learning process and more sensitive to students' needs.

   Sara Edwards in her 1981 study, "Changing Teacher Practices: A Synthesis of Relevant Research," noted a strong correlation between teacher enthusiasm and pupil achievement,[55] and Max Gillett and Meredith Gail supported her finding in their study, "The Effects of Teacher Enthusiasm on the At-Task Behavior of Students in Elementary Grades."[56]

3) **The Eyes Have It!** Effective teachers employ direct eye contact with students. Their eyes are warm and compelling. They also position themselves in the room so that they are facing all students almost all of the time. All of us know that one of the tricks in helping children control their conduct is to be aware of what they are doing.

   In the classroom, however, simple awareness is inadequate. A teacher must know what is going on, and the teacher's behavior must signal that fact to the students. In other words, students must know that the teacher knows what they are doing.

4) **Clarity Is a Clue:** Effective teachers employ clear and concise verbal structures. They phrase questions, directions, and statements clearly.

5) **The Pursuit of Empathy:** Empathy is an important characteristic of effective teachers. They examine a situation through the students' eyes. They listen with interest to student comments and answers, conveying the message, "What you say is important."

6) **The "Raison D'Etre":** Effective teachers include, in each lesson, a solid reason for learning the concept. This "reason for being," or Compelling Why, helps their students realize the importance of applying themselves and learning the concept.

7) **Limiting the Lesson:** Effective teachers' lessons are limited to seven bits of new information at a time, consistent with educational research, and they present the information three different ways — doing, seeing, and hearing. As Woody Hayes said, "walk it, chalk it and talk it." And, students are given a "hook," a way to remember.

8) **Abstract/Concrete:** Effective teachers can explain and illustrate concepts both abstractly and concretely.

9) **Sequential/Global:** Effective teachers know how to teach sequentially and by association; that is, how the concept connects to other concepts.

10) **What Was the Question?:** Effective teachers spend more time on comprehension, creative, and evaluative questions than on memory questions.

11) **KTAV:** Effective teachers' lessons are characterized by a combination of Kinesthetic/Tactual, Auditory, and Visual activities. They rotate their verbs so that the students will see, hear, and feel the concepts being taught.

Effective teachers employ many different methods. When presenting lessons, good teachers use higher pitch for visual verbs, mid-range pitch for auditory verbs, and lower pitch for kinesthetic/tactual verbs. Their hand movements follow a similar pattern.

12) **Checkmate:** Like chess grandmasters, elegant teachers anticipate events in the classroom. Because they can foresee more actions and reactions than other teachers, they can attain a higher level of control in both classroom management and curriculum delivery.

13) **Daydreamers, Beware!** Effective teachers can recognize off-task, tuned out, and daydreaming behavior and act non-confrontationally to bring the student back to attention.

14) **The Last Laugh:** Effective teachers know how to use humor to defuse anxiety and tension.

15) **Counseling That Counts:** In counseling students or parents, effective teachers use positive phrasing,

are empathetic, give support and approval, use problem-solving verbal skills and paraphrases to help people resolve difficulties and think through the possible incongruities in their thinking. They know where they are and plan where they want the conversation to go.

16) **Dyn-O-Mite Dynamics!** Effective teachers are able to direct the dynamics of the group and lead it toward positive goals. They are able to isolate individual and group sources of satisfaction and use them to attain group goals.

17) **If At First You Don't Succeed . . .** Effective teachers can make an error, a misjudgment, a mistake, yet quickly and smoothly recover. They maintain poise when something goes sour. In the event of a classroom catastrophe, they know that they will live to teach effectively another day.

18) **Avoiding Aggravation:** Effective teachers avoid no-win situations.

19) **Variety Is the Spice of Life:** Effective teachers present lessons in interesting, different ways, such as tournaments, simulations, role plays, debates, problem solving, synthesis planning, and metaphorical thinking. The effective teacher uses many different methodologies that promote student thinking while exciting student interest.

20) **The Carrot and the Stick:** Effective teachers use a well-defined reward and penalty system that is both consistent and fair. Intrinsic and extrinsic rewards are used far more often than penalties.

21) **Tactical Emplacement:** In establishing seating arrangements, effective teachers give attention to the relationship of students to each other and to the teacher as well.

Looking back at the teachers we had in school, at the subjects we loved, we can easily recognize that the teacher qualities I have listed very often made the difference. How students feel about the subject matter and the teacher of a class is directly related to how the teacher orchestrates the material.

A Wayne County, Michigan, list of pointers for teachers, circa 1900, recommends "a direct and firm" walk, a "calm and penetrating" eye, and an "elastic and buoyant" nature.[57] Even then they recognized that performance made the difference. Good advice then; good advice now. Yet the question still is, how can we train teachers to develop these, and other, attributes?

In addition to those qualities we have discussed, effective teachers must strive to master teaching tasks, some simple, some complex. These tasks include the ability to deal with student agendas, student resistance, transitional timing, the demands of the clock, the curriculum and whatever current classroom crises arise. Counseling needs must be met, including the need to be able to read body language and interpret tonality.

And teachers have to do all this, even on the days when they're feeling "a quart low," "running on empty," and have just discovered that somebody has swiped the dipstick.

Veteran teachers agree that it is often possible to tell within a short period of time whether a student teacher will make it or not. If they do make it, it will be because of a fortuitous blend of personal characteristics such as warmth, clarity, alertness, and positiveness. The list of 21 attributes of an effective teacher are conclusion statements. The performing moves *produce* conclusion statements like "enthusiasm," "empathy" and "time on task."

The question one must ask is, "Under what conditions does the teacher internalize, best and fastest, the skills of teaching?"

Training the teacher as a champion occurs best when
1) the teacher has the right attributes to teach,
2) the school's vision matches the teacher's vision,
3) the school's leadership style matches the teacher's need for degree of autonomy,
4) the perks of training communicate dignity.

Picking the Talent — If we look at the sports teams or American corporations, they spend an inordinate amount of money on talent selection. We believe that selecting the right talent reduces training time and headaches.

To locate instructors for our courses, we use a talent perceiver developed for us by Selection Research Inc. (SRI) of Lincoln, Nebraska. The perceiver was developed based on the analysis of the common themes of our best instructors. Those themes are:
- Mission
- Achiever
- Command (charisma)
- Stimulator
- Woo (charm)
- Relator

- Innovator
- Discipline (self)
- Individualized perception
- Developer (others)

The advantage of the interview perceiver is that we are more likely to understand the instructor's attributes prior to employment. The interview tends to establish whether or not the educator has a high predisposition for being successful as an educator of teachers. Each of the ten themes are like filling ten glasses—at the end of the interview, we count total volume.

We, in addition, employ all the usual methodologies for selecting talent. The SRI perceiver is one of several screening and selection processes which help us weigh the candidate's predisposition to be successful with teachers.

Whereas our best teacher educators have very different life styles, religious and political beliefs, personalities and demeanors, they tend to share these ten themes. Our best performers tend to respond to questions about these themes in a like manner. There are no 100% guarantees. Yet, like in sports, while some first round picks never get off the bench, and some free agents make all pro, we know that most all pros were top draft picks and almost all free agents are cut from teams after their attributes are evaluated on the field. Winning organizations spend extraordinary effort in talent selection.

If the reader wants to pick staff developers with our perceiver, call us. We learned about the SRI perceiver through some of our clients who use SRI's Teacher Perceiver, which our clients say is very helpful. You can get more information from SRI, Lincoln, Nebraska.

It's my notion that teaching talent can be identified as early as high school, and should be because finding the true talents will be far more difficult in the next generation of teachers. The percentages are high that students with the following qualities may have a predisposition to teach:

1) High energy—they tend to be highly active in many school activities.
2) Bright, happy eyes—the crow lines of eyes tend to be turned up—from smiling, laughing, being positive.
3) Multiple concentration—they tend to read the room well and react well in social situations.
4) Articulate—they are listened to by their peers.
5) Developers—they will make the effort to help others grow.

These teaching talents should be nurtured and given high school classroom opportunities to teach. There should be substantial aid packages for them to go to colleges. They should be linked to our best mentors as school aides for pay throughout their college experience. They should then be linked into a beginning teacher program when they graduate.

Pursuit of Vision — Assuming the talent and training are lined up, it's then crafting the teacher in pursuit of their vision, as closely as possible, to how that fits to team mission.

In my experience, the most challenging management job is crafting personnel to run in the direction they chose to accomplish organizational objectives. The downside is it takes a lot of think time and discussion to reshape functions so that everyone's attributes blend into a cohesive whole. The difficulty comes in having some personnel playing out of position. Is it fair, as an example, to evaluate and reward personnel who agree to play out of position with the same rigor as a person who wants the function?

Smart coaches place players where they think they can do the most good and plan strategy accordingly.

Leadership Compatibility — If we placed teachers on a spectrum from "let me decide," "let us as a group decide," to "let someone else decide for me," we would find educators being highly divergent in their views about authority.

For a host of reasons, some teachers want a strong administration—want the security of prescriptions of how, when, and what to teach. Others are highly offended and antagonistic toward prescriptive controls.

In a district it would be relatively easy to establish the most comfortable leadership style of principals from directive leadership to non-directive. The second phase, then, is to allow teachers to transfer to schools where the leadership style of the principal matches the perceived needs of the teacher.

Education is in gridlock at all levels largely because one person's passion potion is another person's poison. Fundamentally, a breakdown of school morale is largely due to conflicts of control and vision.

In our business, we treat our instructors as inside clients—we do our best to state our vision and bottom-line standards of practice. We state non-negotiables as:

1) Every instructor will communicate high expectations of every teacher.

2) Every instructor will grade every teacher's assignments with comments and will respond to the teacher's comments in their class folder.

3) Every instructor will meet for the contracted period of time with their students.

4) Every instructor will have a student collect evaluations and mail them to PLS for a computer printout.

Beyond that we are a service organization where our instructors are boss. As head of the organization, every time the phone rings, I know who I'm working for—the person on the other end of the line.

At every instructor meeting we underscore that every member of the team is the *integrity* and *reputation* of every other member. It's remarkable how winning teams are built on high expectations of standards.

As a leader, I communicate the vision of the organization and the non-negotiables in tight control. Then, I try to help shape functions so that each player has the independence to use their attributes to accomplish their mission, in a congruent way with students.

Skill development occurs best when people are selected for their attributes to teach. By allowing teachers their preferences in decision control and vision enhancement, and by allowing them to develop congruent skills, they are, therefore, vastly more comfortable to be trained. It is far easier to train a happy employee than a disgruntled one. When selection, vision, and decision control are lined up, we are ready to train the attributes.

I would say to a principal or superintendent, "Teach to a teacher's strengths first." This story illustrates what I mean.

The Animal School — A Parable

Once upon a time the animals decided they must do something decisive to meet the increasing complexity of their society. They held a meeting and finally decided to organize a school.

The curriculum consisted of running, climbing, swimming, and flying. Since these were the basic behaviors of most animals, they decided that all the students should take all the subjects.

The duck proved to be excellent at swimming, better, in fact, than his teacher. He also did well in flying. But he proved to be very poor in running. Since he was poor in this subject he was made to stay after school to practice it, and even had to drop swimming to get more time to practice running. He was kept at his poorest subject until his webbed feet were so badly damaged he became only average at swimming. But, average was acceptable in the school and nobody worried about that. . .except the duck.

The rabbit started at the top of his class in running, but finally had a nervous breakdown because of so much makeup time in swimming. . .a subject he hated.

The squirrel was excellent in climbing until he developed a psychological block in flying class, where the teacher insisted he start flying from the ground instead of the tops of trees. He was kept at attempting to fly until he became musclebound and received a "C" in climbing and a "D" in running.

The eagle was the school's worst discipline problem. In climbing class he beat all of the others to the top of the tree, but he insisted on using his own method of getting there. He received an "F".

The gophers stayed out of school and fought the tax levies for education because digging was not included in the curriculum. They apprenticed their children to the badger and later joined the ground hogs to start a private school offering alternative education.

So the animals held another meeting and criticized the failure of education to produce successful members of society.

If we are going to have a teaching force whose members have internalized practices recommended from the educational research, we have to model attribute development. If we expect teachers to develop student attributes, we have to show the teacher what attribute development looks like, sounds like, and feels like. A champion athlete has one coach who is engaged in ongoing assistance and direction of growth of the athlete's attributes.

Great teachers have the energy to make a positive difference in other people's lives. By training to the attributes we guarantee additional positive energy to make a difference in our children.

Chapter 7

Multiple Concentration

"Those move easiest who have learn'd to dance."—
Alexander Pope

*I*n the last chapter I talked about the characteristics that research has shown effective teachers have in common. That's like analyzing the attributes of all great dancers as smooth promenades, high jumps, and quick pirouettes. Now, strike up the music; the skills that make teachers successful must be performed quickly, and often many must be executed at once. The ballet begins when the bell rings.

While teaching skills are primarily simple and definable, the complexity of elegant teaching arises in the act of combining simple skills in a sequence or using several skills at the same time. This ability, **multiple concentration**, is the cornerstone of elegant teaching.

Multiple concentration is the ability to use the many centers of the brain to process information and, based on that information, to reflexively act or speak with successful results. The brain's perceptual systems continuously collect information to determine what is going on. Flipping back and forth between the various centers, the brain is able to keep track of many things at one time.

A teacher who employs several protocols or skills at the same time, all with precision and finesse, is demonstrating multiple concentration. Your son or daughter demonstrates multiple concentration if he or she has the ability to talk on the phone, watch TV, and do homework simultaneously.

"One of the tasks we're experimenting with is designed to see if expert teachers can process several sources of specialized information simultaneously," David C. Berliner, professor of educational psychology at the University of Arizona, said.

> We set up a task in which the teacher has to monitor three TVs at once. Over on the left is a group of kids, on the right there's a group of kids, straight ahead

is a teacher and another group of kids. The teacher is teaching a lesson on the digestive system using information on an overhead. The question was whether our experts, our novices, and our postulants, could process from all three. It turns out our experts were absolutely unbelievable in doing so. Our first expert had no trouble watching all three screens at once and giving statements about things that were going on and, in fact, kept the sound up on all three screens, which I found absolutely impossible. The majority of experts could not only do it, they could make sense from it.[58]

People vary widely in their ability to perform multiple concentration, covering the entire spectrum on a scale ranging from single concentration to multiple concentration. Some teachers may start out seemingly unable to walk and chew gum at the same time; they probably won't last. Others can do it all, and do it with one hand tied behind their backs while fending off interruptions by the PA system, explaining the Industrial Revolution, and considering whether the eraser that struck the thermostat will cause it to overheat the room and set off the fire alarm and sprinkler system. Whether it is a natural attribute, or acquired through practice, multiple concentration is the single most important attribute of effective teachers.

Juggling the Oranges, Teaching the Class

Metaphorically, if you observed a person singing, dancing, and juggling oranges, all at the same time, you would be observing multiple concentration. Singing involves remembering words and recalling familiar melodies. Juggling oranges requires concentrating on the oranges in the air while catching and tossing them. Dancing is composed of remembering and executing large motor skills. Observing such an extraordinary feat, one has to conclude that the mind is using different centers of the brain to perform all tasks simultaneously.

David K. Cohen, in his 1983 study, "Teaching Practice from the Practitioner's Perspective," alluded to the concept of multiple concentration this way:

Classroom work is typically rapid, and opportunities for reflection are fleeting. There is a great compression of events and few opportunities to stop the music so the teacher can analyze what just happened. Yet these fleeting performances are jam packed. They are, after all, produced jointly by a teacher and at least several students — often an entire class of twenty or thirty. They incorporate complicated interactions around often dense intellectual issues. As a result,...teachers do lots of thinking on their feet...[59]

Cohen went on to say that any analysis being done in classrooms "must be quick," "must respond to particular incidents," and "must shift rapidly from one subject to another."[60]

In "Toward a Theory of Instruction," J.S. Brunner defines this ability as going hand in hand with intellectual development, saying,

Intellectual development is marked by a capacity to deal with several alternatives simultaneously, to tend to several sequences during the same period of time and to allocate time and attention in a manner appropriate to these multiple demands.[61]

If You've Got It, Cultivate It

A predisposition toward multiple concentration is an immense asset for the person who chooses teaching as a career. Teachers who have mastered multiple concentration look smoother and feel more relaxed in the confusion of the classroom than teachers who are limited to a single concentration.

There is no truth to the rumor that beginning teachers who enter the classroom without this quality are found, at year's end, curled in the fetal position, babbling incoherently about hall passes and lunchroom monitors — but it could happen. Multiple concentration is the safety valve quality that allows a teacher not only to survive, but to prevail, helping mold the kind of savvy teacher who not only prevents the classroom pressure cooker from exploding, but uses the pressure cooker to cook to perfection.

An example or two will demonstrate what I mean.

Students are sometimes unruly. John has spent the last half-hour furtively stuffing crayons into the drinking fountain. Raymond has just returned from successfully positioning his textbook so that the school bus scored a direct hit, crushing the binding in the process. Eloise, a sweet little sunbeam, has brought you a flower and wants it placed in water RIGHT NOW! Kevin is wondering, "Can I get this Twinkie out of my Masters of the Universe lunch pail before lunch and take a bite without getting caught?"

Students of all ages, sizes, shapes and colors, whether sweet or stubborn are demanding, expecting, and deserving of their teacher's attention. A teacher with multiple concentration will be able to meet those needs, to water the flowers, quell the raging hormones, quiet the disturbances, and *still* get the lesson across. Kids will see and appreciate such a smooth operator, and love and admire him or her for it.

Such classroom wizards have been born with and have developed a talent for meeting the needs of each John, Raymond, Eloise, or Kevin. Teachers must tap into all such talents, turning them to the tremendous task at hand.

Multiple concentration is a complex mental processing mechanism — and a most important one. The prima ballerina and the professional tennis player possess certain physical assets or attributes which give them the potential to achieve perfection. The basic comparable attribute of the teacher is multiple concentration.

The key to great teaching does not lie in test scores or college grades. It does not come from studying what Dewey did or did not do. Great teaching derives from the teacher's achieved ability for multiple concentration and reflexive execution of teaching skills so learning occurs.

What's Happening In Class

I suspect that no one in teacher development is questioning or discussing what a teacher is processing mentally while in front of a class.

If the teacher is looking at the walls or out the window, instead of reading the students' eyes, the teacher may be performing for herself. Teachers have to be encouraged to *trust* the multiple centers of the brain that read students and events. They have to be encouraged to trust the brain to do simultaneous execution. Teaching is freeform, on-the-feet dynamics. To think that we help this complex, elegant craft by a once-a-year 40-minute gut reading of a teacher's performance is to undervalue the dignity and beauty of teaching.

Training of teachers should be more closely patterned after the training of other performing artists, where training, coaching, modeling, additional training, and more coaching is an ever-perfecting cycle.

We must recognize the importance of identifying and encouraging multiple concentration as a vital asset to survival in the high-speed ballet of daily classroom work. To do less is to do a great disservice to the most important element in our work: the children.

Chapter 8 # Long-Term Teacher Development

"A long pull, and a strong pull, and a pull all together."—Charles Dickens

*L*ong-term teacher development is the trend that holds the most promise for teacher training today.

As Bruce R. Joyce and Beverley Showers have agreed, "One-or-two-day workshops simply do not provide enough time to develop the degree of competence necessary for most trainees to be able to apply a new skill in the work setting."[62]

Writing for Kappan, Samuel B. Bacharach, professor in Cornell's Department of Organizational Behavior, and Sharon C. Conley, said this about educational reform as it affects teacher career planning:

> A genuine career development system for teachers would have as its primary focus the expansion of teaching skills. Unfortunately, few districts give their teachers the in-house technical training that would allow them to upgrade their skills. And without such development opportunities, teachers will continue to feel they are stagnating — regardless of how many bureaucratic 'career ladders' school districts put in place.[63]

We need to make changes in the ways in which teachers are trained. I have some concrete suggestions to improve the areas experts agree need changing. The plan is as follows:

1) New teachers, as a condition of employment, should receive the equivalent of 20 weeks of training and coaching over a five-year span.

2) Forty percent of that training time should be devoted to training the generic skills of teaching, 40% should be devoted to discussion of concrete classroom experiences in a seminar format, and 20% should be devoted to in-class coaching and personalized counseling by teacher educators.

3) One person should ultimately be responsible for delivering a totally proficient teacher. This person would be a recognized teaching expert, such as a retiring Teacher of the Year, a teacher developer, or an outside private or university consultant. The most important concept is, the buck stops here. An equally important concept is, this responsible person must be highly trained, be able to model effective teaching practices, and must be trained as a coach.

4) In most states and provinces retiring teachers leave at twice the salary of a beginning teacher. Between $3,000 and $5,000 per teacher per year over that five-year training period is a totally justifiable and realistic training investment when we consider the amounts that will become available as a result of upcoming teacher retirements.

In addition, it is totally realistic to group new teachers from one or several districts for in-house master degree instruction, under the auspices of a local college. Performance Learning Systems is successfully employing this strategy in several states, in consortia with colleges and districts.

A system should be employed to enable and encourage volunteers to participate in the training of new teachers, to take advantage of the experienced pool of already effective teachers as voluntary mentors.

If there is one observation I can make from our experience of training over 200,000 teachers, it is this: When long-term teacher development plans are put together efficiently and are unanimously supported, everyone wins.

A Win for the School Board

The school board can be educated by the superintendent to recognize the wins that will come to the board from long-term teacher development.

Our national experience tells me that districts can save twice the money that teacher development costs by knowing what works. The best use of district dollars is to employ a training, coaching, and long-term teacher development system that helps teachers internalize the skills used by the most successful teachers.

For the past several decades, business and industry have recognized that when the enterprise takes 100%

responsibility for the employee's skills, strategies, and decision-making abilities — that is, how the employee does the job — employee morale goes up, profits go up, and problems go down.

Schools are profitable when learning takes place, when teachers are confident and competent, and when problems such as dropouts, parent complaints, and student defiance are reduced.

A Win for Teachers

Our experience in working with local and state teacher organizations in teacher development plans has shown:

1) Teachers want more time teaching and less time disciplining.
2) Teachers want a psychic lift from good teaching.
3) Teachers know good teaching is much easier than poor teaching.
4) Teachers want to be proud of their teaching competence, of themselves, and of others.
5) Most teachers recognize that they, next to students, pay for the inadequate teaching behaviors of some colleagues.
6) Most teachers want concrete specific discussion about what skills and strategies work in what classroom and student dynamics/scenarios.
7) Most teachers are willing to invest the time, with management, to improve the working environment.
8) Most teachers prefer *convenient,* practical, long-term teacher development over driving to the university classes.
9) The vast majority of teachers will support the planners of teacher development provided it is a comprehensive package that considers their time to have intrinsic and extrinsic value.
10) Most teachers will eventually buy into teacher development providing they have confidence in the quality of the decision to implement the program.

A Win for School Administrators

1) Administrators benefit from long-term teacher development through a significant reduction of awkward parent conferences where a teacher's behavior contributed to the complaint.

2) A significant reduction of students being directed to the attention of the principal and vice principal for disciplinary action frees administrative time for more positively focused activities.

3) Better teacher attitudes toward their profession will improve administration-teacher communication by creating a positive atmosphere for exchange of ideas.

When teachers and administrators find their jobs easier and more rewarding through training — so will superintendents.

How to Start

To set up effective long-term teacher development, I have found this approach to be most successful: Start by recruiting positive key influentials as an ad hoc committee. I recommend the teacher organization president and chief negotiator and a few others who are well-respected influentials. Honest discussion on the possible, feasible, and desirable should be as open-ended as a dream list. Eventually the discussion evolves into "How do we make it happen?" which connects the teachers to the program.

I have observed three typecastings of teacher organizations:

1) "Who is the president?" — this leadership has such a low-key history its leadership is vaguely known to administration.

2) "The sergeant of arms" — this leadership is characterized by anxiety over any administration decisions. The group is not sure whether teacher development is a negotiated issue or is worthy of organized battle. They anxiously step back and see how the program unfolds. They tend to organize by stonewalling or sabotaging the training more than confronting the district directly.

3) "I'll epoxy your locks" — This teacher organization leadership is the easiest to deal with. Whatever they are angry about is up-front. They want to improve school climate. While they nitpick the details, they deliver on their promises and are very powerful allies over the long term.

Regardless of which stereotype we deal with, the rule is — they have sound reasons of their own to support sophisticated in-district development.

When teacher organization leadership has been identified and the organization integrated into the organizing committee, plan to proceed to larger group discussions, negotiations and/or consensus on a teacher development package for informal presentations to the whole board and entire staff.

See that special attention is paid to guaranteeing early winning experiences in long-term teacher development.

Issue policy statements that say the intent and goal of long term teacher development is to train and coach the teacher to a higher level of effectiveness.

Establish methods to track and evaluate the growth of teachers in training and coaching. Do not, I repeat, *do not* attach teacher growth and coaching to job security evaluation unless the teacher requests it. Your staff development plan is dead if you do. A comedian's gag writer does not judge his success — the audience does; a diving champion's coach does not award gold medals.

What Next?

When the formal decision-makers are in place, they then decide who will be trained. Will it be new personnel only, or all personnel? Will training be given only to those who volunteer, or will it be required across the board?

My opinion is that all new personnel, as a condition of employment, should be trained. Volunteers from among the leaders of the bargaining unit and other key influentials should be part of the training. It is these wielders of influence who can put a positive light on the benefits of training. Administrators, too, should be given high priority for early training. When they understand the training by having taken it, when they are able to use a common skills language with teachers, both groups win.

Making the teacher who is in trouble a forced volunteer in the initial training is a proven error. It is the testimony of other teachers who benefit from training that will help the teacher in trouble cross over and seek out the benefits of training.

I have been in many situations where the administration wants to remedy deficient teachers. While this plan appears good on paper, in practice everyone — including students — quickly figures out who is receiving training and coaching. Training and coaching become associated with being a loser.

My recommendation is, the new and best should be trained first, for two reasons. First, you can get far more growth from your best teachers than you can from the less effective teachers. Dollar for dollar it is a better investment. Second, their enthusiasm is contagious.

I was once asked, "What do we do with marginal teachers on tenure?" My answer is, "You do the same thing you have done for 40 years — ignore them." Let the training itself attract them. If we climb into the minds of these teachers we recognize their sense of helplessness — a sense of abandonment. They probably learned *about* teaching opposite to their learning styles, which means they did not and could not transfer conclusions into performing acts.

The strategy is to make training and coaching so exciting and productive that these marginal teachers begin to hope again, based on their colleagues' testimony. When the voluntary signup sheet comes around again and again, they transfer hope into action.

It saves time, energy, and money to bring the teaching leadership in early and develop the ground rules and implementation plans together, and have the teacher organizations persuade their membership. I have yet to see this formula fail.

When we at Performance Learning Systems go to a district, one of the first questions we ask is, "What is the board's relationship to the collective bargaining unit?" We get answers from, "A marriage made in heaven" to "They eat nails before negotiations."

One of our non-negotiable conditions is to meet with the president and a few officers of the union. We ask them if they consider in-school teacher development to be a condition of employment issue. Why? Because there are too many ways for teachers, as individuals, and the bargaining unit as a group, to stonewall cooperation.

I could fill a book with stories about districts that had very little rapport with the collective bargaining units, where suspicion and double-crosses were the rule. We have found in every case where concrete teaching skills are discussed with a fair approach high on the agenda, that the bargaining units are much tougher in their expectations of a businesslike approach by their own members than the board would be.

The teacher organizations and their members are tired of cut-and-paste inservice, tired of one-day inservices, tired of courses in double talk and double think. They bluntly want performing solutions to complex teaching scenarios. What is often forgotten is: Every classroom blunder is paid for by a teacher and by the staff as a whole.

When a district says to teachers, "We are willing to invest in this training, provided you are receptive," it starts a dialogue of win-win.

Simply stated, collective bargaining units are powerful allies once the policy is clear and fair.

What and Who?

What will be trained? Specific skills and reflexive execution training to produce world-class champion performers for our classrooms should be the intent of teacher development.

Who will do the training? If the decision is made that insiders will train teachers, those selected for this important role must be well-respected models of sound teaching practices. Benefits of using insiders are that they are already on the payroll, they know the inside political structure, and they have a power base, which can be a big plus.

On the other hand, outsiders are unincumbered by past history. They cost more, yet can be more easily released. They do not know the inside political structure, and they do not have a power base, which in some districts is a plus.

My professional opinion is, the district should employ and train the best teachers of teachers. Both instructors from outside and inside the school should be sought out and interviewed.

Benefits A District Can Expect

After five years of long-term teacher development, a district can expect the following benefits:

1) Vandalism reduction visible in dollar amounts
2) Student absenteeism reduction visible in dollar amounts
3) Teacher absenteeism reduction visible in dollar amounts
4) Reduction of specialists due to upgraded teacher proficiency visible in dollar amounts
5) Teacher evaluations based on specific skill executions showing steady improvement
6) Upward changes in student test scores
7) Administrator and department head observing favorable improvement

When long-term teacher development plans are put together efficiently, and unanimously supported, everyone benefits. I stress that the superintendent, and through his or her influence the school board, must support such long-term teacher development to ensure its success.

A superintendent will find that supporting long-term teacher development contributes to his or her own job security by improving the quality of teaching in the district. The superintendent is the determining factor in improving the district. He or she must sell the board, find the money, and foster a professional esprit de corps with teachers and their representatives.

Long-term teacher development can be a factor in creating improved morale and spirit within a school district. Team spirit can be nurtured by identifying influential educators within a district and appointing them to ad hoc committees which conduct open, honest discussions on possible improvements. Just as an effective classroom teacher must work the group dynamics of his or her classroom, so, too, must a superintendent strive to lead educators toward a common vision.

It is a collaborative approach that ultimately decides if the long-term teacher development will be limited to voluntary participants only, mandated for all staff, or apply only to new personnel. It is my recommendation that the district require all new personnel to take part in long-term teacher development for the first five years as a condition of employment. It is our opinion that beginning teacher programs are "high leverage activities," as I will explain in the next chapter.

In summary, long-term teacher development will have important benefits for these ten reasons:

1) Teachers welcome concrete "nuts and bolts" suggestions about what skills and strategies will work with which children in their classroom.
2) Successful teacher development is profitable, as proven in industry. In Search of Excellence and Passion for Excellence, two books which are recommended reading for school executives, prove this.
3) Esprit de corps: A clearer sense of the group mission is fostered through participation in long-term teacher development.
4) Absenteeism among teachers and students alike declines when esprit de corps exists. Absent teachers and students cost a district money.

5) Dropouts and vandalism, two costly propositions, decrease in a district where a sense of mission is present.

6) As teachers increase in proficiency, fewer special service teachers are needed, thereby saving the district money. The savings for lowered rates of vandalism, absenteeism, and increased teacher proficiency can be passed along to the working teacher.

7) Teachers want and need the psychic lift they experience with good teaching. Good teaching is infinitely easier and more rewarding than ineffective teaching. Better teachers spend more time teaching, less time disciplining.

8) Good teachers pay both psychologically and economically for weak or poorly trained teachers.

9) Courses taught within the schools are practical and convenient, when compared to a college or university commute.

10) If all employees in a district "speak the same language," it provides a common denominator to aid in coaching and evaluation efforts.

Teachers will invest in long-term teacher development once the benefits are proven.

The profession of teaching is too elegant to be relegated to mediocrity. How to train the great teacher has been determined through research and experience in the field. We must articulate clear performance patterns. Training and coaching must be present. A competent teacher *can* be guaranteed.

Now is the time to consider the merits of training teachers as performing artists. Now is the time to discuss certifying them as competent professionals in the field. Now is the time to begin a new day for a new generation of teachers and teacher educators.

Chapter 9 # Coaching

"The reasonable thing is to learn from those who can teach."—Sophocles

*I*n our own organization, I get coached after every presentation. Why? Because I need it. Also, I have to be secure enough to allow myself to be coached, modeling that coaching starts at the top, as corporate policy. Every Performance Learning Systems instructor in the field gets coached several times a year by a colleague. As an organization we pay for our teacher educators to coach each other. Why? Because we know that two heads are better than one.

Every person in our organization has two or three areas of performance on which they are working. Mine are organizing directions into steps, and rotating my KTAV verbs in stories and explanations. I'm doing this because pros are coached. As the CEO, what I do is the message.

Coaching to a high level of proficiency must be an integral part of any development program. It is especially important to teacher development plans.

A good training program that teaches specific classroom skills can be compared to planting seeds. When the seeds are tended with care, nurtured, and encouraged to grow, the planting will be successful. Coaching is long-range cultivation and, as such, is an essential part of any teacher development program whose aim is long-term internalized learning. Without coaching, teachers tend to revert to previous practices. Ongoing coaching helps them to persist in using new techniques.

Based on our experience in scores of districts, I have concluded that the research is correct. If you give a teacher only knowledge, you can expect a five to ten percent impact. That means only 10% of the skills are transferred to the teacher's repertoire.

When you provide the specific training *and model it,* you increase the use of the skill to 20%. Practice in the training class and in the classroom doubles it again to 40%. If it ends there, the teachers have taken away less than half of the potential training.

When teachers are provided with *coaching,* the proficiency again doubles — to 80%, and keeps climbing as the coaching continues.

Coaching provides support to those teachers who might otherwise drift back into less effective patterns if left without encouragement. The mere training of a skill does not ensure transfer into an active repertoire and regular use. Coaching helps teachers transfer new skills into their repertoires and refine existing skills.

Making Coaching Work

It's one thing to be an opera critic and entirely another thing to train the opera singer.

The reason teachers resist many coaching plans is that what is called coaching is often evaluation of conclusions, without specific concrete suggestions on what performing moves will produce desirable results. It lacks the honesty of being helpful.

Teachers will accept and support long-term teacher development once they see that their coaches are on their side, helping them to succeed. To accomplish this end, the coach and the evaluator must be two different people.

As the coaching begins to pay off, the teacher demonstrates that he or she has automatic command of the generic skills of teaching and also can use good judgment in deciding which skill to execute in which situation. Joyce, Showers, and others agree with us that, "Skills have to be overlearned so that they're past conscious thinking."[64] Automatic execution of appropriate patterns in each situation is the desired goal. Coaching can help achieve that goal.

As with football players who must throw a block or execute a tackle during a football game without conscious thought, teachers must know the generic skills of teaching so well that they will automatically choose the correct performance pattern and use it. Coaching, which is a superior form of practice, can help teachers gain that sort of automatic competence.

Actors, pilots, surgeons, all respect the coaching they receive. The teacher's trainer and coach must be a person with extensive successful classroom experience who can read the subtle intricacies of classroom situations and make specific, concrete suggestions.

Teachers want concrete, specific information about what skills and strategies work in what classroom scenarios. As an example, teachers know from the research and from experience that positive practice is better than negative. They want to know how to apply it to a student who cheats, makes smart remarks, or shoots paper clips.

Just as the vast majority of teachers will support teacher development plans, they will support coaching provided it is designed to help them master the specific skills of teaching. They are weary of one-shot miracle cures that evaluate results before they have had a chance to learn the skills and performance patterns.

Martina Navritilova, the world-class tennis player, gave great credit to her coach because he trained her to reduce wasted motion in fundamental moves with her arm and leg motion. In a parallel way, teachers can be trained in skills like rotating their verbs and activities to cover all preferred learning styles, to reduce the wasted motion of teaching.

There are three elements common to successful performing artists and their coaches:

1) The teacher/coach is clearly on the same team or has a positive client relationship with the performer.
2) The focus of the teacher/coach is mostly on honing basic skills and performance patterns, especially early in a career.
3) The judge, evaluator, critic, clearly should be someone other than the coach.

Four-Level Approach to Coaching

In a recent newspaper editorial, readers were cautioned that when discussing and deciding upon political issues, they must consider whether they are discussing *vision, strategy, tactics,* or *operation.* The same four levels are important for the coaching of teachers. The editorial writer provides the following definitions:

> At the level of *vision,* we are simply creating in our imagination the end result. *Strategy* involves a broad plan on how to achieve it. *Tactics* involve plans to achieve particular parts of the overall goal. *Operations* involve the execution of tactics.[65]

Let's consider defining each of the four levels within the school setting:

1) If the schools are to be successful in achieving their missions in society, and in educating students, there must be agreement among school personnel at the

instructional and administrative levels as to the mission or *vision* of the school system.

2) When coaching a classroom teacher, *strategy* could be defined as the curriculum, or unit of study.

3) *Tactics* may be analogous to a lesson plan that attempts to achieve a small goal related to the overall strategy.

4) Finally, *operations* would include the teacher's teaching skills and behaviors used to execute the lesson plan. Operations include skill and performance patterns which are used in consortia to accomplish tactical objectives.

There has been much discontent from both school administrators and teachers about the real value of most teacher evaluation systems. Many administrators have noted a strong teacher resistance and antagonism when feedback points out the failure of a teacher's execution. This strong resistance may be caused in part by the teacher unconsciously relating negative feedback to disapproval of the teacher's tactics and strategy. Maybe, even more significantly, personalizing the comments is seen as disapproval of the teacher's vision.

As an example, the most positive attribute of one teacher may be high ability in counseling. Another teacher may be high in technical skills, such as classroom questions and lesson delivery. Their strengths will affect how they pursue the common vision. If administration values one tactic over the other, the teacher is seen as a good teacher in one area and inadequate in the other. Both may well be contributing strongly to the vision, but in differing ways.

Consider how much more positively and openly a teacher might respond if the necessary communication took place with acceptance and approval of the teacher's mission, validating that the strategy was logical and the tactics appropriate. With those assurances in place, a teacher might be much more willing to accept coaching feedback to improve his or her performance, as a means of achieving the teacher's vision.

Of course, a problem may exist due to a teacher's implementation of inappropriate tactics or strategy; or, an even more difficult problem, the teacher may approach the classroom with a vision that is incongruent to that of the evaluators. In such a case, feedback concerning the teacher's performance is of little value, as it could not possibly create the necessary change.

Consideration of these four levels may encourage teacher observers to dedicate the necessary time required to totally involving the teacher in the evaluative/coaching process. Also, teacher coaches need to develop the necessary communication and questioning skills to identify the vision, strategy, and tactics behind the teacher's lesson, before commenting on the operations.

Who Should Be Coached

As I mentioned in the beginning of the chapter, a willingness to be coached starts at the top.

Realistically, the next question is: where does one start a coaching program? The answer is with beginning teachers. Why? You can catch them in "reality shock" and help them succeed.

Some of the most frequently reported or observed problems of beginning teachers are:

a. disciplining students (by far the most prevalent problem)
b. motivating students
c. dealing with individual differences
d. assessing student work
e. relating to parents
f. organizing class work
g. obtaining sufficient materials and supplies
h. dealing with problems of individual students.

All of the above statements are conclusion statements requiring "how to" skills. All teachers, regardless of years of experience, essentially have the same problems as beginning teachers except they have learned to cope by "playing the game" long enough. This does not mean experienced teachers play the game well. It means their classroom experiences illuminated into generalizations that avoid disasters or produce success — if the teacher has a strong inductive mind.

A person can learn to play golf or tennis without lessons on fundamental skills and strategies, yet everyone knows trained players can beat the socks off untrained players. While teaching is not a contest, we still have winning and losing when it comes to student learning.

A strong linkage into staff development is through a beginning teacher program because it ties experienced teachers (coaches) to beginning teachers. The best coaches also have strong developer themes. This means they are going to get "hyped" working and developing a new teacher. These experienced teachers may or may not be the best in the district, although they're always highly respected. The cutting question in finding developers (coaches) is: who will invest conscientious time in their own improvement and the improvement of others?

The entry point for a strong staff development program may begin with 20 coaches and 20 new teachers in a district of 200. This is a 20% start in building credibility with the other 160 teachers (80%.) The doubters of an effective program are doubters for good reasons. They have had too many bad experiences with their own anger about their own coping with reality shock.

The reason why having mandatory beginning teacher and voluntary (yet rewarded) coaches as a starting point to whole staff development is that it's the easiest way to get support by the collective bargaining agent. Our surveys show that the majority of teachers would support mandatory staff development, under certain conditions, yet leadership faces an ever-present vocal minority who could call "sell out" in "terms and conditions of employment." This could cause loss of membership. A bargaining unit is more likely to support a mandatory program for beginning teachers as a starting point than having to later monitor success without threatening the security of the collective bargaining unit.

Steve Barkley, veteran teacher coaching trainer, points out the danger of focusing coaching first on teachers who are having problems.

> A Teacher Assistance Team is put in place to work with teachers having problems. If you have a good team, within a year they've solved all those problems. So then the school board says, 'This Teacher Assistance Team idea really works! Why don't we send them to some other classrooms?'

> Think about the mental attitude of the competent teacher who walks into class one morning. . .and there is the Teacher Assistance Team! Coaching — called Teacher Assistance — has acquired a negative mindset. Teacher development has become a deficit.

> Coaching is not just for the novice or the teacher in trouble. Coaching is rewarding to everyone. Look at

all the highly effective teachers, the top of the profession. The reward for these teachers is continued growth through observation and positive feedback.

School districts must place more emphasis on coaching the best people in the system, to get away from the deficit model of teacher development. If you look at the private sector, the greatest personnel development dollars are spent with the best people in the company. Why? Because they yield the greatest return. So, when a district invests teacher development dollars in the top teachers, those teachers give that much more back to the system. The strongest teachers on the staff learn the fastest and get the most from coaching. Their example will attract other teachers.

Teacher evaluation, on the other hand, is concerned with minimum standards, not with the technical skills the highly experienced teachers have developed. The most incongruent thing happening today is that increasing excellence in education is being talked about in terms of increasing the *minimum* standards! Could you imagine a hospital taking out a full-page newspaper ad guaranteeing that doctors practicing in the hospital are those who meet the minimum requirements for a medical license? I think not. [66]

One of our instructors, Diana Ramsey, recalls working with a man who had been teaching for 13 years and had decided to leave the profession. The teacher took a workshop to consider alternative careers for teachers. Two days into the workshop the teacher reported, "They described for me all the skills I've developed in the last 13 years that are marketable. I'm so impressed, I'm going to stay in teaching!"

"The problem was," Ramsey said, "in more than a decade of teaching no one had taken the time to identify the technical skills this teacher was developing. This is the heart of what coaching has to offer the advanced teacher."

Therefore, the strategy of who should be coached falls into the following order:

For the first year, all new teachers and an equal number of mentors in a three-to-five year program.

In the second and third year, as credibility grows, we have found collective bargaining units highly cooperative in guiding good volunteers and teachers in trouble into training and coaching to "fill out the class" and take advantage of the perks. The perks are the rewards for the teacher: free tuition, salary barrier credit, trips to conventions, or straight pay. However, first and foremost, the district and trainers and coaches have to develop an intrinsic reward ethos that communicates that great teaching is self-rewarding. We have found collective bargaining units who agreed off the record to modify next year's salary demands to reward people who invest time in staff development through pay incentives, to the detriment of people who reject staff development. Therefore, over time, the contract erodes the real income of those who refuse self-improvement and rewards those who do invest in themselves and others.

Who Would Coach?

Modeling and coaching are the most powerful transfer techniques available to produce internalization. For the transfer to take place the mentor/coach has to have the capacity to see meaningful discriminations, and have the wisdom to isolate a teachable moment with good advice. The coach must know the specific skills of tonality, body language, and word structures that have been trained, and all the options for performing those skills.

Madeline Hunter has said that a coach is a person who has the skills to enable another person to perform better. "Coaching takes special knowledge," she added.[67]

Who should coach? Ideally every teacher would help coach every other teacher in a district in a helpful spirit of give-and-take. Realistically, educators and coaches should have a predisposition for self-improvement as well as a desire to help develop others, and be highly enough trained in the width and depth of skill patterns and options to be completely helpful. While it is most helpful to be coached by proven professionals, the economics of this model is expensive. If the district coach, observing during an off period, is considered "free," and the outsider expert cost is considered as a consultant fee, obviously the coaching by district people is far less expensive. At the same time, there are risks in using first-time people in any venture.

With insider or outsider coaching plans, the idea is to encourage a teacher trying to improve his or her skills, especially in the early stages of learning new performance patterns. The skilled coach knows that when the teacher is concentrating on new skills, other already internalized skills are lost for a time. It is usual for the teacher to be too busy worrying about his or her own performance to read student response to his or her efforts.

Anyone can evaluate the way a sportscaster or movie critic performs. . .what's good and what's not good; it's another thing to coach the champion to a successful performance by helping facilitate the learning and internalizing of skill and performance patterns. And, most important, by knowing *what, when,* and *how* to coach. Great coaches, in my observation, say very little, yet when they do say something it is specific and simple.

Joyce and Showers note,

> On a practical basis, most coaching should be done by teams of teachers working together to study new approaches to teaching and to polish their existing teaching skills. There is, of course, no reason why administrators or curriculum supervisors or college professors cannot be effective coaches, too. But if only as a matter of logistics, teachers are closer to one another and in an excellent position to do most of the coaching necessary.[68]

Joyce and Showers make it sound as if these groups are qualified to coach. I'll leave this section with a question: If it takes ten years of internalization for a person to judge cattle at a county fair, how much training is required to coach or judge teachers? In our own experiences with coaching plans, we don't yet know if it is more cost effective in results to have a trainer work with twenty teachers or to train twenty coaches to work with each other in consultation with the trainer. The cost/yield answer is speculative as of this writing.

Dealing with Changes

The Swami From Miami, a San Francisco radio comedian, once said, "Change is the most important thing in life. Without it you cannot do your laundry."

Seriously, the coaching process, when implemented, must have the proper climate if it is to be successful. In most cases this involves change in the system.

"In most situations, coaching involves change in the school system. Progressive leaders must learn to manage the paradox of change," Gary Holtzman, a Pennsylvania educator, has written.

> Change often requires a creative destruction of what has worked in the past. Change is often threatening and frightening to people within the organization. Our school leaders must demonstrate that change can be stimulating and exciting.

> The first step of change is the felt need for change. The pressure to bring about change in the school program may come from external forces, such as the Carnegie Report, the school board, or a parent group, or it can occur from within, from the administration or faculty. During this first stage, school leaders must provide strong support and assurance.

> The second step involves creation of a vision to guide the change. This response to felt need for change should predict positive benefits and seek staff support and commitment. The final phase of initiating change should come only after careful preparation, when faculty and administration are mentally ready. This phase requires shaping and reinforcing the vision to fit the organization. All involved must be continually reminded of the commitment that has been made.[69]

Coaching Requires Trust and Commitment

Trust is paramount on all levels. This demands an openness and willingness to take risks on the part of all within the organization; trusting each other to share decision making, trusting each other enough to put egos on the line, and trusting each other to break down the barriers that exist in a school from one classroom to another. This type of trust takes time to build, but when it occurs there is an energy level within the district that is exciting and fun to be around.

The second essential factor is commitment from the top down. It must start with the superintendent, the CEO of education. It is his or her responsibility to sell the program and gain commitment from the people in the organization. If the people in the organization see that the superintendent is willing to take the risk, they will too. As the head of a substantial organization, I felt the same trepidation in front of a group as many people feel when I asked to be coached. First I said, "You have been watching me work. Please coach me on my delivery. What did I do well?" After receiving the responses and thanking participants for their comments, I ask, "What could I have done better?" Again I thank the people for their comments and let them know that I'll work on their suggestions. Then, the next time I work with the group, I say to them, "I would like to work on the suggestions you gave me the last time we met," which I do. Eventually, people give the greatest compliment of all, "You are what you do," because they see the congruence of my actions.

In addition, I often will videotape myself working with a group. I find teachers are much kinder and more generous in their comments and suggestions than I am of my teaching competence. Videotaping is a powerful medium for self-coaching as well. I have found it helpful to say out loud, "I forgive myself. I'll do it better next time." And, I often do improve the next time.

When We Support Teachers We Stimulate and Affirm Them

To promote excellence we must strive to reshape the environment into one conducive to professional growth. Cooperative coaching fosters openness, trust, and good communication — removed from the evaluative process. Teachers must be able to confront their own strengths and opportunities for growth in an atmosphere free from the threat of subsequent evaluation.

When a teacher takes a tennis lesson from a pro, the teacher pays the coach. The teacher is the client, the coach is the consultant. The combined effort is the strengthening of the game for the teacher, because better playing is more rewarding. This is the attitude that has to be transferred: "I work with my coach to continually practice for greater precision in my game."

Coaches help teachers reflect on progress and offer suggestions based on their expertise in the skills being learned. Coaches become teammates with teachers working toward mutual goals of skill attainment. The coach is a key facilitator for ongoing change. This dynamic creates opportunities for teachers to celebrate other teachers.

I like the following definition of coaching, as formulated by Pennsylvania's Cumberland Valley School District:

"The process of coaching is an ongoing collegial relationship which takes place in a supportive environment where increased awareness of learning principles and teaching strategies encourages....educators to achieve their highest potential; resulting in optimum student learning."

Coaching brings teachers together to work on common instructional growth. Coaching provides interpersonal support and reduces the sense of isolation many teachers feel in the classroom.

Coaching is an important process that offers the following benefits to the classroom teacher:

1) A coach provides empathetic companionship for a teacher attempting to master new classroom performance patterns.

Joyce and Showers note that, "It is tragic that teaching currently provides so little interpersonal support and close contact with other teachers, because classrooms are terribly isolated places. Coaching reduces the isolation and offers genuine support."[70] They feel that "continuous practice, feedback, and the companionship of coaches is essential to enable even highly motivated persons to bring additions to their repertoire under effective control."[71]

2) Coaches provide valuable technical feedback. The coaching is nonjudgmental — the atmosphere should be more that of a "cheering parent" in the stands than an evaluator with a clipboard. Coaches help the learner by pointing out opportunities.

3) One of the things a coach can help a teacher do is to read the signals of the students, so that the correct response from the teacher is guaranteed. "Two heads are better than one" in this and many other areas.

4) There is another important element present in successful coaching — modeling. When a coach models a skill the opportunity is provided for the teacher to see the skill correctly implemented. It is often easier to see these opportunities when observing someone else, rather than when you are the one mastering the new teaching skill. Teachers say the lack of modeling is one of the greatest crises involved in teacher education.

Coaching a teacher to achieve the best, most consistent use of new skills makes good sense. As you may recall from Chapter Three, providing the greatest number of changes per dollar invested is very important. Coaching provides an opportunity to double the district's return on the training investment. The intrinsic payoff for teachers is that good teaching is easier and more fun than bad teaching and gives the teacher dignity in the profession.

Chapter 10

Isolating What Is to be Trained

*"**train** 1. To coach in, or accustom to, some mode of behavior or performance. 2. To . . .become proficient with specialized instruction and practice."—American Heritage Dictionary*

*T*he critical incidents of a rural British Columbia classroom are the same as those of a New York City classroom. The frequency and intensity may be different, but the incidents are the same. Pushing, hitting, and swearing occur everywhere.

Walk into any school building anywhere, including the worst neighborhoods, and you will find winners who can cope, and losers who just mope. Some teachers are far more effective with problem students than others. Why? Follow those "golden" teachers around and find out why they are succeeding while others are failing. If we carefully listen and observe, a set of skills and strategies used by expert teachers will emerge. The list of skills will bear out education research. All you have to do to get the gold is go to the bank; tap into the expert teacher treasury.

Starting in 1971 Performance Learning Systems began examining teaching in terms of skills applied to classroom scenarios by interviewing outstanding teachers. We found the top teachers by asking collective bargaining units and school district personnel, "If your child were in trouble educationally, to whose classroom would you send him or her?"

Then we asked these teachers why they had the "magic" and why they had "magic" beyond others. We taped case-study role plays to see how they handled various critical incidents. What we sought were operational/functional skills and strategies.

Along their career paths teachers accumulate mental pictures of anxiety-producing scenarios like the dreaded smart remark and the intimidating, irate parent. We wanted to find out how the best of the best had solved these situations.

Skills for the Performing Art of Teaching

The next step after identifying the critical skills of teaching was to design a performance pattern that could be internalized, to make each skill reflexive.

Before we go on, let's define skill and performance patterns. A skill is a predictably successful verbal structure to a classroom scenario. For example, an Open-Ended Question — one of the identified verbal skills of teaching — invites a larger response from this student. "Janie, how did you reach that decision?" A Closed-Ended Question limits the student's response to essentials. "Harry, how much time do you need?"

The execution of a skill involves a number of additional factors, such as warmth of eye contact, congruent body language, and appropriate voice tonality.

Our investigations of great teachers showed us that teaching is conducted best with specific verbal structures that are clear, concise and correct to classroom episodes. Body language and tonality must be congruent in the execution of the skill.

We found that 90% of what an expert teacher says fits within these interactive skill structures, except for information frames where the student asks a question and the teacher responds.

The following skills have been consistently identified through the observation of successful teachers in grades K-12 and verified through the study of educational research. They represent 225 hours of training in Performance Learning Systems courses Project T.E.A.C.H. (Teacher Effectiveness and Classroom Handling), P.R.I.D.E. (Professional Refinements in Developing Effectiveness), TEACHING through LEARNING CHANNELS, Patterns for I.D.E.A.S., Motivation (in development), and The Parent Teacher Conference.

This list of over 160 skills represents the continuous findings of Performance Learning Systems since 1972. Our best educated guess is that there are more skills to be discovered as we continue to learn more about teaching.

Keep in mind that each skill has verbal structures, tonality, and body language that accompany it. Each skill has multiple applications to classroom scenarios — the teacher "reads" teaching events as they unfold, the teacher then decides what skills (options) might work, chooses one, and performs the skill in a cause and effect network. This is parallel to chess moves. The teacher is both a cause and effect performer and thinker.

Skills for the Performing Art of Teaching
As taught in the Performance Learning Systems course
Project T.E.A.C.H.

Verbal Skills for Positive Classroom Management
Training Hours
30 hours
- open-ended questions
- closed-ended questions
- confirmatory paraphrase
- leading paraphrase
- positive phrasing
- empathy statement
- supporting statement
- approval statement
- problem-solving inquiry
- contingency action proposal
- disapproval statement
- authority statement
- P.O.W.E.R. judgment

Concentration on Sustaining Momentum
10 hours
- issue conversion
- irrelevant maneuver
- humor
- guardian gambit
- advise me tactic
- encroachment name dropping
- encroachment eye contact
- encroachment moving in
- transitional timing
- tactical emplacement
- random questioning
- student accountability

Concentration on Team Building and Being a Natural Leader
5 hours
- pride process
- trophy process
- share-a-secret process
- VIP process

Skills for the Performing Art of Teaching
As taught in the Performance Learning Systems course
P.R.I.D.E.

The Art of Questioning	Training Hours
Modes of Questions	7 hours

memory
comprehension
    interpretation
    analysis
    application
creative
evaluation
    personal
    generic

Clarity   2 hours
ask the question to be answered
leave out parenthetical words
ask one question at a time
use age-appropriate vocabulary

Pause Periods   2 hours
before calling on a student
after calling on a student
after student answers

Probes   2 hours
memory
comprehension
creative
evaluation

Responding to Student Answers   3 hours
avoid repetition
paraphrasing
correct answers through praise and
   approval
incorrect answers
partially correct answers
"non" answers
taking responsibility

**Reading Student Nonverbal
Communication**
warmth   8 hours
astonishment
attentiveness
concentration on task

thinking about it
recurrent nervous behaviors
self-consciousness
hesitancy
control
distancing
shyness
facial
inquiry
perplexity
disguised perplexity
tiredness
daydreaming
tuning out
doubt
disbelief
sullenness
silent challenge
overt challenge
acting out
confrontation stance

The Nonverbal Communication of Teachers
positive nonverbal signals   6 hours
enthusiasm
involvement
self-confidence
congruence

Motivating Change in Student Behaviors
Increase behavior through rewards/reinforcers   10 hours
appropriate
sufficient
vary rewards
given after
immediate
intermittent
contracting
escape reinforcement
Decrease behavior
penalties
nonreinforcement
restitution
Critical Incidents in the Classroom   5 hours

Skills for the Performing Art of Teaching
As taught in the Performance Learning Systems course
TEACHING through LEARNING CHANNELS

Modality Preferences	**Training Hours**
visual	15 hours

auditory
kinesthetic
tactual
learn to assess teacher preferences
learn to assess student preferences
teaching lessons to meet the
   four modality types through
      eye movements
      verb rotations
      voice pitch
      hand movements
      color
      light
      identification of kinesthetic,
        tactual, auditory, and
        visual teaching strategies

Organization Preferences of the Brain

sequential organization	9 hours

    analysis
    classification
    deductive reasoning
    inductive reasoning
global organization
    synthesis
    stories
    deductive reasoning
learn to assess teacher preferences
learn to assess student preferences
teaching lessons to meet the two
   organization preferences of the brain

Conceptual Preferences of the Brain	Training Hours
concrete	9 hours
visuals	
sounds	
feelings	
body movements	
abstract	
written words	
spoken words	
numerals	
equations	

learn to assess teacher preferences
learn to assess student preferences
teaching lessons to meet the two
   conceptual preferences of the brain

Concept Development

similarities	6 hours

differences
labels
operating
combining
learn to use all five processes and
   incorporate them into the
   conceptual development of
   students

Long-Term Memory

the "compelling why"	6 hours

memory hooks
   visual
   auditory
   kinesthetic
   tactual
seven "bits" of information
three repetitions

Skills for the Performing Art of Teaching
As taught in the Performance Learning Systems course
Patterns for I.D.E.A.S.

	Training Hours
inductive statement	30 hours
inductive enquiry	
deductive statement	
deductive enquiry	
analysis statement	
analysis enquiry	
synthesis statement	
synthesis enquiry	
supporting statement	
issue statement	
proof statement	
problem/solution statement	
summary statement	
synthesis suggestion	
sensory and relationship patterns	
auditory	5 hours
visual	
olfactory	
gustatory	
feelings/emotions	
tactual	
kinesthetic	
cause and effect	
sequence	
uses	
proportions	
physical parts	
value	
stories	
hierarchy	
step-by-step progression	10 hours
label imaging	
music memory hook	
estimating	
prioritizing	
predicting	
word mapping	
skilled discussion	

Skills for the Performing Art of Teaching
As taught in the Performance Learning Systems course
The Parent Teacher Conference

The Five Phases	Training Hours
warm-up	15 hours
positive attributes	
presentation of student growth	
parent-teacher collaboration	
closing	

These then are performance moves, i.e., verbal structures, tonality, and body language skills which, when internalized, cause student learning independent of grade level, subject, philosophy, or curriculum approach. While the frequency of use and professional judgment of teachers may vary, the performance pattern is the same. When we look at a creative, Olympic ice skater, the flow of the performance is different according to the music and the routine. What remains the same is the skill precision that composes the leaps, jumps, and turns. The same principle applies to the cause and effect network of classroom skills to produce desirable conclusions.

A Cause and Effect Context
The application of skills to all classroom interactions will be demonstrated, in part, throughout this next section. Keep in mind, we became interested in educational research conclusions to establish a connection between our operational-functional skill model to "live classroom scenarios." We found that the expert testimony of our expert teachers is 100% consistent with educational research and adds the "how" to the "what" of classroom scenarios.

The following story illustrates the difference between a teacher's emotional classroom reaction — mine — and what should have been a reflexive skill execution.

I first met Steve in a stairwell. I pulled him away from a fist-fight with another boy who seemed twice Steve's size. As a result of the fist-fight Steve was suspended from school. The next time I saw him was the following term in my math and science classes. We got along pretty well, in spite of some typical junior high school defiance. Sometimes, though, I question the methods I used to deal with his rebelliousness.

Once, for example, when I gave an assignment in class, Steve burst out in a loud hostile voice, "Fun, really fun!"

There were several ways in which I could have responded to prevent the escalation of this incident. I could have used a Leading Paraphrase, saying, in a calm, matter-of-fact voice: "Your tonality is appropriate to your words." I could have chosen a Confirmatory Paraphrase: "You have mixed feelings about the assignment." Positive Phrasing might have served well: "When you get into the assignment, you may find that it's fun." A touch of humor, a warm smile, and a lift of the eyes might have done the job: "The tone of your voice tells me that you'll love it." I could have used a calmly stated Disapproval Statement or an Authority Statement. Some teachers might have chosen nonreinforcement, ignoring the comment.

The discrepancy between what I might have done and what I did do was large. I shot right back at Steve, equally loudly and harshly, "Look, Steve, if you don't like what's going on here, leave." Steve walked out, and I was left with two problems — my class's momentum had been destroyed by the outburst, and one of my students had gone off to parts unknown! My lack of precise skill training had cost me. The story continues.

Ten years later I was sitting in a restaurant when I heard a voice call, "Hey, Mr. Hasenstab. How're you doing?" It was Steve. He told me he had left school to open a gas station, and then had opened a second one. He had later completed high school and gone on to college. By the time he ran into me, he had been accepted at law school and was selling his gas stations.

I asked him, as casually as I could, "Why were you in trouble with all those teachers in junior high school?"

"Oh, that," he answered. "They were scared of me, and they didn't like me. They were always in the hall saying things like, 'Poor Stevey, poor boy, his mother died right in front of him on a class trip in fifth grade.' They were afraid of me and yet trying to comfort me at the same time."

From what he told me about his behavior and his teachers' actions and reactions, I was able to construct a composite of how teacher misbehavior can cause student misbehavior.

Steve would show up in class full of energy. He had a lot of friends and a loud voice. The students would speak to each other, and Steve would make remarks to friends across the room. The teachers, biased by "Stevey stories" in the teachers' room, were alert to "future pacing," i.e., potential "Stevey problems." The teachers' anxiety was visible and was very clearly recorded in Steve's right brain. Tensional tonality is also registered there. From the moment his teacher walked in, Steve could read tension in her face, her eyes, and her tone of voice.

Looking back on those years, I can recall seeing the tension in the teachers' bodies increase when Steve approached them in the hall. They tightened up visibly, unaware of their reactions. Steve saw the tension.

I hasten to add that these were very good teachers and fine people. In his heart of hearts, Steve realized that when thinking of him as "poor Stevey" the teachers were moved by compassion.

On the other hand, Steve felt that he had reconciled himself to the loss of his mother, and he was angry that people thought his problems were caused by his mother's death. Steve felt that his teachers were patronizing him. Every time he stepped out of line, his counselors and teachers would say, "We know how difficult it must be."

If Steve's problems didn't stem from his mother's death, what did cause them? Steve knew that he had been a very angry youngster. As we spoke over coffee, he explained, "The teacher would begin the class and one of the kids would do something silly. The teacher would say, 'Charles, get to work.' I'd meddle and say, 'Yeah. Get to work, Charles.' With a forced smile, the teacher would plead, 'C'mon, Steve, open your book.' I'd answer, loudly, 'Why should I?'"

Steve's confrontational reaction would trigger the teacher's fight-or-flight response — the hypothalamus triggering the pituitary to release hormones into the blood stream causing the heart to beat faster, blood pressure to rise, blood vessels to dilate, muscles to contract, the hair to stand on end, and the bronchial tubes to open for deeper breathing. When a teacher is feeling the pressure, it's highly visible. Steve saw the incongruity between his teacher's intended message — her sweet tone of voice, her mothering, her positive words — and the tension in her face and the fear in her eyes.

What did Steve get out of his behavior? The reaction of his teacher, which was inadvertent misbehavior.

"She'd force a smile and say through clenched teeth, 'You have to open the book because that's what we have to do to get on with the lesson.'" The teacher imagines a blowup, imagines Steve's march to the Vice Principal's office, imagines the explanations, filling out the forms, all the other things. And all Steve would say is, "It's a dumb lesson anyway."

Steve was one of those healthy, wisecracking, bantering students who challenge our leadership resources and skills. In a positive sense, he communicated, "Don't tread on me." After Steve and students like him practice on us, they often become attorneys, negotiators, politicians, or entrepreneurs. Their bantering and outspoken verbal skills are important for the success of our society.

Perhaps the most important question raised by Steve's story is, "Are teachers being trained to handle critical incidents with students like Steve in a positive, reflexive, and professional manner?"

Skills Make the Difference

As the education research now shows, skills and performance patterns are what make the difference in teaching performance, as they do for performing artists like pro quarterbacks, surgeons, pilots, comedians, jazz players, and orchestra conductors.

Just as a pro quarterback reads a defense, a teacher reads a classroom. Just as a surgeon diagnoses illnesses and executes his craft, a teacher reads class problems and teaches to correct them. Just as a pilot gets an airplane off the ground, keeps it in the air, lands it, and is reflexively trained to handle emergency situations, so too the teacher must handle tricky 50-minute classroom flights.

Just as the comedian uses story, wit, timing, and upstaging the environment, so does the teacher. Just as the jazz player has a freeform style based on precise execution in relationship with other players, so does the teacher with the students. And finally, the effective teacher, like the orchestra leader, leads everyone toward a cooperative and elegant result.

All of these performing arts, including teaching, rest on finely honed skills and performance patterns, including complex decision-making while in the act of performing. Instead, almost all of a teacher's education is designed as if the teacher is a spectator, not the performer. It's hard to imagine pro quarterbacks, surgeons, comedians, jazz players, pilots, and orchestra conductors being trained as spectators, and then performing without skill and performance training and coaching.

The purpose of this book is not to criticize the twenty to thirty thousand teacher educators who serve as staff developers. Nor is it to criticize teacher training institutions or regulators of teacher training programs. They, after all, have provided the programs and executed their best judgments, according to the decisions of their predecessors tracing back at least a half century. Teacher education has traveled down a 50-year path of seeing teaching only as an academic pursuit, *not* seeing the teacher as a performing artist.

One purpose of this book is to place in the hands of those dedicated educators and staff developers the best, most current thinking about proven techniques to enable them to do their difficult jobs of making our teachers the most effective educators possible.

Implications of Skill Training to Education Research

The future of education research would be greatly enhanced by synthesis research. Synthesis research, because of clearly defined skills, allows scores of teachers at various grade levels and subjects to experiment and estimate efficiency and results of various lesson formats. Synthesis research allows a lesson designer to develop a concise format of skill "how to's" with basic time frames. These formats can then be disseminated among teachers who have the same internalized vocabulary. They can then take the concise format and slug in the current content. They deliver the lesson and report back. This is precisely what PLS did in designing PATTERNS for I.D.E.A.S. Participants in these experiments were either instructors or were highly recommended by instructors as having internalized the skill patterns. We first requested "magical lesson formats" from teachers, that is, lessons that perhaps for some unknown reason worked. We processed these formats into variations which field teachers experimented with, reporting results back to us in various subjects and grade levels. We found consistency in what worked well. The cornerstone of the development of PATTERNS for I.D.E.A.S. was the precise meaning of skill definitions understood by all educators involved in the research. The value of common vocabulary in the performance "how to's" produces the opportunity for synthesis research. The value of having clear limits and bounds in skill definitions was what produced consistent observations when the original "Format A" was compared to a later version of "Format A" with slight modifications. The consistency of quality control helped us take positions with confidence. The point is that skill training has positive implications to the professionalization of teaching and efficiency of student learning. If skill training works, what is the difference between what should be and the existing structure?

What's Being Done in Teacher Education Isn't Working

Here's an example that points out how badly the present systems are failing. We asked 500 teachers in three states to respond to a word association exercise by writing the first image that came to their minds. The words the teachers were asked to respond to were "inservice," "staff development," and "graduate education courses."

More than half the responses were hostile and negative. About a third were mixed images, and the remainder were generally positive. Teachers often are hostile to staff development and inservice when the instruction proves to be superfluous, unnecessarily time consuming, or counterproductive. Their attitudes could best be summed up as, "Don't waste my time with this stuff unless it will help me to teach better tomorrow morning."

Making the Abstract Concrete

When teachers seem confused by suggestions others make for their improvement, it usually is because the suggestions are abstract when they should be concrete. Most teachers interpret abstract theories as intellectual featherbedding. Teacher educators need to understand that practicing teachers are saying "so what" to every phrase the teacher educator is spouting. It is not only imperative to throw out every abstraction that does not meet the "so what" criterion, it is also better to throw out those that are difficult to articulate.

The 1986 A.S.C.D. Yearbook points out vividly that the experts have marched a long time in the direction of abstract conclusions, vague generalizations, and educationese. As an example, the Yearbook asked eleven experts what kind of feedback they would give teachers. They visited and observed teachers and wrote coaching feedback to the teachers. All the responses, rather than being concrete and specific to any execution, were vague and abstract. This excerpt is typical:

"[Teacher's name] could be encouraged to think about these perspectives, about teaching and the teacher's role in schooling in general, and to consider the findings from Goodlad's 1983 study, the results of Little's 1981 investigation of workplace norm associated with school success, Eisner's

1985 propositions about curriculum evaluation, and Raywid's 1984 study of schools of choice. These attempts to understand schooling might trigger a sense of empowerment mentioned earlier."[72]

I emphasize that as well-intentioned as the advice is, it's hardly helpful to a teacher. If you think that it was good advice, consider the quarterback at half time, or the surgeon in an operation working around a set of vital nerves, being coached to the library for readings.

All of the eleven experts dealt at the conclusion level using what they knew to be the best approach and technology — *of fifty years ago!* What has been going on in teacher training, and is still going on, is technologically obsolete, according to education research.

The classroom teacher wants concrete specific help in the same way ballet students get help with specific moves.

It is probably as difficult for a history, sociology, philosophy, psychology, or research person to cross over to skills and performance pattern training and coaching as it would be for a sportscaster to become a coach, or for a movie critic to become an actor.

"Go F— Yourself!" and Other Words of Wisdom

I remember a teacher educator who was comparing various education theorists on a highly abstract level when a teacher interrupted, "I had a student tell me to go f— myself. Can you tell me how I should have responded?"

The teacher educator said, "Well, I would have to know the individual differences of the child as compared to others, what motivated him, and then I'd have to take a holistic approach to his problem."

The questioner shot back, "I'm sinking while you're waffling. Now respond as if I'm the student!"

The professor flushed red with anger and said, "You don't have to be here; you can leave."

The teacher responded, "Well, you know what I did? I sent the kid to the principal, and the principal sent him back."

The professor lost the critical incident and the entire class of teachers as he returned to reading his lecture.

Since any theory is just educated guessing on an abstract level, it is vital for the teacher educator to be able to convert theory into practice, making concrete suggestions for the classroom teacher based on the available research.

The professor should have gained a context for the misbehavior from the teacher and made simple verbal suggestions for various responses to the student, such as the following:

(Note: the correct tonality and body language have to be imagined by the reader.)

"Your words are appropriate to a school setting." (Leading Paraphrase) — stated calmly.

"In this classroom we learn to speak with civil words and tone, even when we are legitimately angry. We will discuss this incident after school in the presence of your father." (Authority Statement) — stated matter-of-factly.

"You are angry and hostile." (Confirmatory Paraphrase) — stated with concern.

"Why are you hostile?" (Open-Ended Question) — stated quizzically.

"For you to stand up to me takes a great deal of courage." (Approval Statement) — stated warmly. "I've had bad days when everything upsets me, too. You are going to have to reorganize your ideas so that you express them in a civilized fashion." (Empathy Statement) — stated compassionately.

There are several additional ways the teacher could respond. Knowing the conclusion we want is easy. Knowing *how* to achieve the conclusion is what the teacher wants and needs.

Advice or evaluation at the conclusion level is not very helpful. We must deal with observable behaviors that are specific, not vague conclusion statements such as "he's disorganized," or "needs to stay on task," or "is distractable," or even "has difficulty with peers." There are *specific behaviors* that compose these generalizations. Teachers need the specifics if they are to bring about the conclusions.

Another typical piece of advice to teachers is that they should ask more complex questions. What they never get are the "how to" of the 27 skill and performance patterns that compose effective questioning.

As an example, the technically correct way to ask a question is to use pause time after the question, before calling on a student, to allow time for thought. Another pause should happen after the student's answer to allow the answering student to provide additional information.

How to respond to correct, incorrect, partially correct, and non-answers are skills that must be exercised reflexively. The same is true of knowing how to probe the student for a fuller answer and how to listen to student answers. Clarity is an important aspect of good questioning skills. More complex questions such as comprehension, creative, and evaluation questions require that the teacher know the beginning words. These performing skills can be taught in 20 hours. It also requires hundreds of hours of conscientious effort to reflexively deliver a sound proficiency.

"Skills to situations" is how the mind most efficiently operates. This means that the mind is engineered to produce thinking for live scenarios. The mind analyzes an event, compares the event to other events (inductive), identifies likely skills to handle the event (analysis), and then the body, through action, handles the event (synthesis). The result is mentally video taped to access success for handling future events (analysis and induction).

This principle is true for efficient internalization of all learning, including K-12 learning. The criteria for learning is not pencil and paper tests; it's what the person *does* when faced with a live situation. Our "beef" with teacher education is that if "skills to situations" is the most sound pedagogy for all learning, it must be modeled so teachers can feel the difference of skills to events compared to conclusion statement learning.

Yes, But Will It Work?

If teachers see the practicality, the "compelling why" of new proficiencies, they will work to develop them.

Doyle and Ponder conducted a 1977 study on teachers' perceptions of the "practicality" of teaching tactics. They concluded that if a teacher perceives a practice as difficult to implement or lacking congruence with his or her preferred teaching style, he or she is unlikely to use it.[73]

In a 1982 overview of the research on inservice effectiveness, it was found that ". . .the program's relevance is the more important of these factors [for teacher enthusiasm] and that even mandatory programs may eventually be accepted by teachers when the classroom outcomes of the new approaches are sufficiently effective."[74] Likewise, a "Follow-up Evaluation of an Inservice Programme Based on Action Research" found that the long-term success of professional development programs depends on the quality of the original offering, coupled with availability of support services.[75]

Results Must Vastly Exceed the Investment

The time and effort spent to learn to internalize teaching skills must have probable time and energy savings for the future. Who wants to spend considerable time and effort for small gains? The trick of effective teaching is to spend little effort for large gains. Do people invest in anything where the capital start-up costs are enormous and the yield small? An educator's time is not free, and unlimited time is not available.

The problem for staff developers is that staff development gets grouped in with other innovations. For example, one innovation perceived by many as being doomed to failure is writing performance objectives on every lesson and sometimes for every child. It didn't work in Michigan or New Jersey, so why would it work in Indiana? While it looks good on paper at a school board or PTA meeting, teacher effort far exceeds the student benefits. Teachers claim that what is charted as an objective today does not apply or is forgotten by next week, next month, or next year.

These teachers ask, "Was the documentation worth it? Was this worth all the effort?" These sorts of tasks contribute to a feeling of frustration and futility, a feeling of being trapped on the educational treadmill. Often, good teachers wind up saying, "Stop the treadmill! I want to get off!"

Dodging the Dirty (Paper) Work

In the real world of teaching, teachers do one of three things to cope with treadmill activities that require much time and effort and produce little yield. Faced with a demand to "write minimal competencies," or "write performance objectives," or any of a myriad of other such myopic mucking about, they will take evasive action in an effort to "dodge the dirty work."

Many teachers work the extra hours on the paper shuffling while anger and fatigue set in, depressing their performance during class hours. Many negative comments heard in teacher lounges have originated with red tape and busy work that take away from a teacher's real task — teaching.

Or, they will procrastinate and become anxious and guilt-ridden, sometimes even depressed in their class performance.

Some will find a way to plagiarize in the spirit of passive resistance, and worry about getting caught. This approach also depresses performance. Often, teachers group sound staff development with other reforms which have proved not to work.

It is in this context that teacher educators and innovation planners have to be very careful in screening the ideas for teacher education reform by identifying "compelling whys," "so whats," and results versus efforts.

There are five essential functions a teacher trainer must perform to get the best return from the district's investment in teacher development:

1) Isolate the critical incidents and then decide what works in the classroom, that is, what separates a successful teacher from an unsuccessful one.
2) Define the performance moves clearly, by function.
3) Be concrete. Avoid abstractions.
4) Be certain that the performance solutions trained are the correct solutions to the problem.
5) Ensure that results are cost-efficient. Results should vastly exceed the time and energy invested.

What Are You Really Saying?

One of many serious problems with teacher education is the lack of a clear-cut definition of skills and a rationale showing the benefit of those skills.

Skills are only useful tools in a network of cause and effect applications. Definitions of terms, skill performance steps, and rules for probable application have to be clearly understood by all concerned.

"Your time on task would improve if you asked more complex questions." Unless all concerned have agreement on skill definition and execution of "time on task" and "complex questions," how can the teacher improve?

We know empathy is a good skill — research proves it is better for a teacher to show empathy with students than not. The point is how the teacher communicates empathy. As we isolate what is to be trained, we must keep the emphasis on the *execution* of the skill.

Time on task consists of over 40 skill and performance patterns, and questioning involves 27 skill patterns. So, unless the teacher knows the "hows" of time on task and complex questions, the result is forever out of reach.

What We Want Is High Performance

The great flaw of teacher education, training, coaching, and evaluation is that it may be totally out of sync with what we know about performing artists and education research. If the evaluator who makes the conclusions is not trained in the skill and performance patterns, including a common language, no standard of practice exists for teaching conduct.

Contrast this with all the performing professions, where the standards of skill and performance are highly defined and well known. We've all seen the network sportscaster covering the Olympic figure skating competition. The sportscaster usually is flanked by a retired skating champion who rattles off the skills and rates their performance, trying to beat the judges to the punch for the television audience.

In teaching, the standards of skill and performance patterns are now highly defined. But there are few who know them, let alone who are able to train, model, and coach them.

When we look at the great teachers and see what they do to make teaching work, it becomes clear what must be trained. The skills and strategies they have forged into gold from the bitter metal of daily classroom struggle have been analyzed.

When clear, precise definitions of the skills have been built and teachers are given compelling whys for their use, and when the skills have been laid out with clear descriptions of their relation to each other, followed by training in their application to typical and high-impact scenarios, teachers will transfer from the vision of sound practice to the execution of sound practice.

Assessments of expertise must include both skill in the art and craft of teaching as well as theoretical knowledge and critical acumen, Stanford University's Elliot Eisner told a symposium on expert teaching.[76]

Bottom line: The skills the teacher reflexively applies count for at least as much as academic knowledge in the art of teaching. Without the wheels of performing skills, the cargo of knowledge may go undelivered.

Chapter 11 Modeling Is Teacher Training that "Takes"

"Example is the school of mankind, and they will learn at no other"—Edmund Burke

---

*T*he most effective teacher training method is modeling. Modeling a practice demonstrates what is being taught. What is taught becomes believable when a model uses it elegantly, and the teachers feel the synthesis on their own motivation and learning. That is the point at which the first step transfer takes place.

For instance, an instructor is giving teachers examples of positive phrasing, and at the same time *using* positive phrasing in her exchanges with the teachers. "She is teaching us the precise skill as she uses the precise skill. I want to try it on my own kids."

In this way, teachers are involved in the practical teaching agenda in a close, use-oriented way. Abstract, word-oriented talk sessions are not adequate to change behaviors.[77]

The goal in teacher development is to build an elegant teacher who really, deep down, "knows" successful teaching practices. To accomplish that goal, those who instruct teachers must be models of all the desired teaching skills. When we ask why some teachers have succeeded in learning effective teaching methods where others have failed, the answer is always, "great modeling made the difference."

Modeling has been identified as the most effective teaching method.[78] One researcher said, "It is emphasized that modeling desirable behavior is a primary responsibility for teachers at all levels. . ."[79]

Equally important, if not more important, to a district's progress is administrative modeling. The more that administrators in a district model the importance of professional growth, the more others in the district will recognize that such activities are valued and important.

Our collective willingness to accept changes in teacher education such as modeling-based instruction *is* a form of modeling: we are modeling our openness and our desire to improve.

As the teacher educator faces the class of teachers for the first time, it relieves anxiety and models good teaching methods to say to the class, "I will take responsibility for your learning and will re-teach it in as many different ways as is necessary for you to get it. The only thing I will expect from you is a positive attitude, so that you keep working until you can execute it as well as I do."

By using different ways to explain concepts, the teacher educator will be modeling what a teacher's attitude should be with every student: "I'll keep changing my approach until you have it."

Modeling is the message. Of that we are sure. At one time in education, a "role model" meant the school district forbade teachers to drink, smoke, or chase the opposite sex. By contrast, the new modeling means exhibiting the execution of proficiencies identified in the research and observed in the most elegant teaching performers.

The "Real McCoy": Recognizing Teaching Excellence

Teachers and administrators alike have to experience what good teaching looks, sounds, and feels like. When teacher educators adroitly model the skills they want their teachers to mirror and master, internalization is facilitated. Good teaching is the highly observable execution of fundamental skills with precision and finesse.

As an example, I once watched an elegant presentation by a teacher trainer to an audience of 150 curriculum coordinators, administrators, and teachers. The audience sensed the quality of this presenter's performance. After the speech, the presenter was asked, "Can we learn to use our hands and to move across the floor as you do?"

She answered, "Yes, definitely." She was right, because elegant teaching is every bit as definable as elegant acting, singing, gymnastics, or diving — all performance arts.

A Good Example

Stephen Barkley of Performance Learning Systems gives the following example of the importance of modeling.

"I enrolled in a course called Individualized Instruction. There were 250 of us in the auditorium. Someone read notes from a lectern. About the third hour into the program this little beeper went off in my mind. I realized that if individualized instruction was so important, how come we're not doing it here!"

Another story comes from Geraldine Flaherty, one of PLS's veteran instructors.

"I was called into a school and asked to do a workshop on creating a trusting environment. The teachers had to sign into the workshop and sign out. There was nothing I could do to overcome the powerful negative model of what was to be taught. Management was modeling the non-trust of teachers and asking them to model trust of students."

Modeling is *doing* what we believe — it *is* the message. So, it's vital that the coach and the school environment model the message, whether it's "Individualized Instruction," "trusting," or "coaching/mentoring."

"Eureka!" Moments

Nadia Comaneci, the Olympic gymnast whose exploits we cheered at the Los Angeles Olympic games in 1984, fired the imagination of a generation of children who aspired to her elegance and perfection.

In every performing field, to model elegance is to create the desire to emulate. When members of the audience asked the lecturer, "How can we learn to do what you have done?" they were expressing the desire to internalize what was being demonstrated by an elegant model.

When students emulate professional athletes' behavior, such as spiking the ball in volleyball or giving the "high five" after a basket, the students have learned by imitation. A Little Leaguer steps up to the plate, taps the plate twice with the bat, touches his cap, swings twice, and awaits the pitch. He repeats the ritual for each pitch. The coach doesn't teach those behaviors. It's a ritual learned by imitating models. Similarly, teacher proficiency internalization will vastly improve when teacher educators become models of proven proficiencies.

What we model is the message. We have designed modeling into Performance Learning Systems courses as an important communication component because we want teachers who take our training to internalize what they have learned. Research, field testing, and our ongoing training experience have shown us that internalization is faster and more complete when the training instructor models the concept as it is explained. The ultimate test of our motivational power is how well they perform when we're not there.

If the professionalization of teaching is to occur, it is vital to first train all teacher educators to model sound practice. How else can we be believed?

Chapter 12

Sending Teachers to Class

"Greater than the tread of mighty armies is an idea whose time has come."—Victor Hugo

Y ou've read why I insist on seeing the teacher as a performing artist — because that's what teachers are. You've stayed with me as I described the ways we observed and identified skills used by the best teachers. You can see the sense in training all teachers to be as effective as the best teachers in the profession.

It is now appropriate to share some "nuts and bolts" about what to expect when teachers go to class.

Training Climate

The psychological climate of teachers being trained, even under the best of circumstances, often ranges from defensive to "wait and see." Generally, teachers join the class prepared to enter a "safe" relationship, that is, one characterized by polite distance. They frequently want to maintain the safe relationship throughout the course, never moving beyond it to a trusting relationship.

Like students, teachers bring to class different sets of resistances and hidden agendas, most of which they are unwilling to reveal. Some they may not even realize they possess. Often, teachers reveal these resistances through "leakages," unwittingly exposing their vulnerabilities and fears both verbally and nonverbally.

Teacher reluctance to reveal these hidden agendas is understandable. Should they open up to the teacher educator and to their colleagues who will judge them as fellow teachers? Should teachers share their occasional sense of inadequacy, their mistakes? If they do, will they still feel comfortable and confident in a teacher education class? We say definitely yes. It can be made to happen if the teachers are secure in the knowledge that their course grade is unrelated to their classroom practices, past or present.

Admittedly, teachers are in a double bind when they reveal themselves. If a teacher has hit a student for swearing, is that teacher going to ask for an alternative solution from a person who is in the position of grading her or his performance? Not likely — unless she or he trusts the instructor and the other members of the class.

Overcoming Resistance

The vulnerabilities (resistances, hidden agendas) that most teachers have at the beginning of a course can be expressed in the questions they silently ask themselves:

1) How do my teaching practices compare with those of others in the room?
2) Will I lose face if I'm wrong? Will I look silly? Will I expose a prejudice that people will hold against me?
3) Will people in the class pass the word around that I'm inadequate? Will they label me a poor teacher?
4) Can I invest time and energy in trying things? I've been led down the garden path before with half-baked ideas that ultimately failed. Can I believe again?
5) What is really wrong with what I've been doing? Is the course content implying that I'm incompetent?
6) Who is this instructor anyway? Is he or she better than I am? Why should I trust a self-proclaimed expert?

Everyone has these first-day doubts. That is why the seats at the back of the room are always filled first.

We carefully observe teachers as they enter Performance Learning Systems classes, seeing how they relate to others, and how they relate to us.

A teacher might say, "What do you do when a student refuses to hand in homework?" If the teacher is hesitant, asks the question in measured tones, and seems to want to talk about "someone else's" student, a safe relationship exists. If the teacher says, instead, "I have a defiant student who refuses to hand in homework and I get really angry at her," and there is emotion in the voice and free use of "feeling" words, we are in a trusting relationship.

Initially, almost everyone will enter into a safe relationship, except for a few people with exceptionally high self-concepts. Those individuals may go right into a trusting relationship. By the third to fifth session, safe relationships will change to trusting ones.

That is why picking instructors is a most vital function. They must have multiple concentration. They must be people who can read the situations in the room. The teacher educator has to be highly competent to read and motivate teachers.

In coaching instructors I notice that the great ones assure the class members that it is a cooperative relationship. The instructor will share unsuccessful experiences from his or her own career to move teachers and instructor toward a common human level.

An astute teacher educator will recognize the hidden agenda and respond to neutralize the fears and apprehensions. The goal of the teacher educator should be to move the teacher from a safe relationship to a trusting one. An instructor in one of our courses told me, "I know how successful I've been based on the number of gut issues teachers share with me during in-class discussions and in one-on-one counseling sessions before and after class."

It is the instructor's responsibility in character, demeanor, and execution to produce a learning climate that makes teachers comfortable with their own skills. This is very different from normal graduate courses where the information is far removed from the everyday practice of teaching.

As the skills are taught and modeled, teachers warm to the new tools. Increasingly they see the tools as important solutions to their own teaching problems. It is usefulness that makes the critical difference.

"All complex learning that requires concentrated effort over time depends on intrinsic motivation," notes an article in Phi Delta Kappan."[80] "Extrinsic motives alone are not enough to cause students to identify with a body of knowledge and internalize it."[81]

For students of a subject to genuinely engage in that subject, the teacher of that class — whether it is a class of eighth graders or a class of teachers learning how to teach — must be able to overcome resistance to the concepts being taught. This is the first challenge. An excellent teacher trainer meets the challenge by skillfully orchestrating the training climate.

The bottom line in overcoming resistances of any kind, in any class, at any level, at any time, is to model proven teaching methods. Modeling the skill and performance patterns of championship teaching in a warm, responsive, and human way opens the door to learning.

Trust-Building Strategies

Until there is trust there will be little learning transferred. To assure the class members that they are in a cooperative, not an adversarial situation, the instructor might say at the first session: "I'm here both as a helpful coach and as someone who will evaluate your work. Grades are based on your attendance and effort in class and on completion of assignments.

"Attendance is, of course, your being present at every session. Effort is your best attempt to learn the practices being taught. Your effort is observable as concentration, attentiveness, and willingness to try new skills. Completed assignments are judged for clarity and completeness.

"Your grade is separate and distinct from how I might perceive your teaching practices, your classroom control, or your opportunities to grow. You may have the greatest room for improvement and still get an 'A' if you meet the criteria. Your grade is independent of whether you agree or disagree with me. Disagreeing and agreeing are evaluative processes. Both are positive forces for learning. I'm here to coach you in the precise refinements of teaching so your job can become easier and more enjoyable. Anything that takes place here, anything that is said, is held as confidential by me and everyone present. If we are going to solve real problems, it is important that we all feel safe and can be honest. (Five-second pause.) Agreed? (Five-second pause.) Then we agree that we are all free to express ourselves on real issues and real problems. We hope to leave here with real solutions."

Some teachers will accept this immediately. Others will take a wait-and-see attitude.

At least once every three sessions the instructor should share an unsuccessful experience from her or his own career. It should be done with genuine humor. At the end of the story the instructor should say something like, "I'm a pro. I forgive myself." This strategy is very effective for getting teachers to relax and become more comfortable with looking their teaching opportunities squarely in the eye.

It is important to emphasize the fact that all professionals are coached. Once every three or four sessions the instructor should say something like, "Placido Domingo is a professional, world-class opera singer. He is coached. Paul Molitor is a professional baseball player at the top of his career. He is coached. Mike Tyson is the World Heavyweight Boxing Champion, and he's coached. I'm a professional. Coach me. How can I improve?"

A participant might respond, "You teach pause time, yet I notice that sometimes you cut in immediately when someone is finished giving an answer."

A good response to that might be, "I know I have a problem with pause time and I'll work on it. Thank you." This is the power of modeling.

Nonverbal signals, both sent and received, can be used to build trust. Seeing a look of concern on a participant's face, the instructor could say, "Mary, you have a concern."

"No, that's O.K."

"If you had a concern, what would it be?"

The wording fits the third-party word structure of the safe relationship. Instructors report that they almost always get a positive response and a look of ease when the concern is handled this way. This modeling works in any classroom.

Disagreement can be handled tactfully. For example, "Mary believes that students should follow the teacher's directions because that's the way it is in the work world." This should be said with one open palm facing upward and toward Mary. "Ted believes that we have an obligation to help students to learn to make independent decisions." This statement is accompanied with the other open palm being presented toward Ted, followed by a brief pause. "Perhaps both points of view are important." Both hands are then brought together and clasped in a conciliatory gesture. Those who use this training technique maintain that they have yet to experience a continued argument once their hands have been clasped. This performance pattern, that works in teacher education, will work in the teacher's classroom.

In a situation where a participant is strongly at odds with accepted educational practice, the following technique may work.

Teacher-participant: "Listen, I use the 'reach and teach' method. When a kid gets out of line I reach for his collar with both hands, pull him close to my face, and then I teach him."

Instructor: "That works and you have no side effects such as student resentment." (Stated calmly) (Leading Paraphrase)

Teacher: (Defensively) "I keep control."

Instructor: (Calmly) "How would you know whether your way or our way produces better short- or long-term results?" (Pause) (Open-Ended Question)

Teacher: "I'd have to compare the two methods."

Instructor: "Would you feel like trying?" (Closed-Ended Question)

The Training Site

In addition to the human factors, it is important that everyone involved know exactly how important the physical surroundings can be to internalization of the proficiencies being taught and to overcoming class resistances.

Ordinarily, training occurs in whatever room is available, such as a school cafeteria or campus classroom. The rooms often are stark, communicating coldness and institutionalization. The seats are uncomfortable.

Most teachers acquiesce, in the same way that most New York subway commuters accept their surroundings as a condition of getting to their jobs. To make teachers enthusiastic participants in their training, their surroundings should be pleasant, clean, and comfortable, with ample writing space and good lighting.

Certainly teacher training should occur in the best room available in the district — it communicates priority and respect.

Amenities

Amenities are important to the psychological well-being of individuals and the dynamics of group training. The breaking of bread as a communal act is timeless. When people break bread together, bonds are built.

We recommend clients develop training rooms that have a full kitchen with a stove, a full-sized refrigerator, cabinets, and a sink at the back of the classroom. This communicates more than the availability of beverages and food; it communicates motherly love. It anchors training with family ritual. You can see far more warm conversation when teachers are treated as V.I.P.s. By contrast, a seminar where the breaks lead to the water fountain and lunch is a quick bite at a fast food place, produces what it projects — coldness.

When people have the comforts of home, with a kitchen, the classroom conversation and debate are more civil, tolerant, and reflective. When trainees are minus the amenities, the conversation is more "public place," direct, impulsive, and less civil. While this might appear to be acceptable, the sponsor has to recognize that internalization of training behaviors is anxiety-producing by itself. Lack of amenities adds to the resistance because the dynamic is less civil, more cold. Experienced trainers, public and private, say amenities make an observable difference in the quality of interaction and internalization.

Training Time

If the district and university sponsors want the most ideal time for internalization of skills to occur, the training should be scheduled during daytime hours in the summer.

Performance Learning Systems did a computer survey of the course ratings of several thousand participants. The composite average evaluation was "73% Excellent" over several thousand evaluations. The following numbers show the internalization success of various time slots.

Time of Day		Spread
3:30 - 6:30	- 8%	-18%
6:30 - 9:30	- 3%	-13%
During Day	+10%	Day Base

The reasons for the statistical differences are speculative, yet common sense may invest these figures with meaning.

The 3:30 - 6:30 time slot is the worst because often teachers are anxiously driving to the site, exhausted from five hours of high intensity teaching. They are hungry and wondering what they will have for dinner. The sudden realization that they have forgotten to thaw out dinner, the dog won't have anyone to let him out for his evening constitutional, or that they are going to have to go directly from class to Sally's band concert or Johnny's basketball game with no dinner. . .is Migraine City.

The 6:30 - 9:30 time is somewhat better; still the fatigue of the day is highly visible as it approaches 9:00 p.m. The less interested members of the class will be stifling yawns and digging their fingernails into their hands to stay awake. If Sam is ticked that he is missing Monday Night Football and Sue is regretting missing the new TV mini-series, the instruction doesn't stand a fair chance.

The season when training occurs also makes a difference in internalization.

Season		Spread
Fall*	+3%	-7%
Winter/Spring*	- 6%	-16%
Summer	+10%	Summer Base

*Note: After School

Based solely on the time of year the training is given, fall semesters are much better than spring semesters. Teachers recognize that new or more highly honed proficiencies are a better investment in the fall. In the spring, emotionally, educators are counting the days until summer, as are their students. Weekend training results have an 18% point advantage over after-school training.

To have maximum internalization, the one-or two-week summer session is most efficient. Daytime training during summers is vastly superior, as are weekends during the rest of the year. The time of day and the time of the year both affect teacher evaluations and it is our belief that those two factors also affect internalization of skills.

Historically, teacher education takes place after school and in the evenings because the costs both in substitutes and lost student learning time are thought to be nonnegotiable. Our experience is that teachers prefer choices — weekends, summers, or after school.

Rituals

There are certain rituals that help the training process to be successful. The most important executives sponsoring the training should give a brief welcome and/or closing. This communicates priority, mission, and importance.

The unspoken message is, "I came here today to communicate to you the importance of this training session to our mission as a school district. Each of us affects the lives of our children and the future of our society. This training session will help you to increase your proficiencies in our vital mission of making the children of today everything they can be as the adults of tomorrow. To that end we have placed extensive resources at your disposal to aid you to become everything you can be."

It is highly desirable that the training session end with some form of celebration. A potluck supper, a punch or wine-and-cheese party, cracking a bottle of champagne, or attending an elegant formal dinner are all suitable celebrations of achievement. These activities foster warm companionship.

We tend to celebrate with those we like, those we trust, and those with whom we have bonds. Celebrations reinforce the priority of our mission.

The positive learning qualities of the site, the quality of the training time, the amenities and rituals, all have a profound effect on the internalization of what is taught. A thoroughly professional staff developer will make these seemingly secondary training aspects a primary concern. They will prove to be extremely useful methods of advancing the major strategies of overcoming resistance and building trust.

Chapter 13

Evaluation of Elegant Teaching

"You can have a craft without an art, but you can't have an art without a craft."—Ansel Adams

W e have talked about the proficiencies — the skills that must be internalized for a teacher to be great. Now, let us consider how to best, and most fairly, evaluate the use of those proficiencies.

"Judging teaching is absolutely no different from judging figure skating, poultry, potatoes, or cows. Each involves making complex decisions with a good deal of subjectivity," David C. Berliner, professor of educational psychology at the University of Arizona, said in an interview.[82]

> The difference is practice. It takes 15 years to become an Olympic skating judge. We all marvel at the reliability of the judges as we look at the Olympics every four years. That doesn't just happen. Those people have 20 or 30 years under their belts learning to do that — but our state departments of education pick new people every year and give them little or no training.[83]

Training to become adept at evaluation is essential. For instance, the evaluator must know that teachers' already internalized skills will decline in proficiency temporarily while the teacher concentrates on a new skill.

A well-trained evaluator will know that some teachers shine more brightly than normal when their class is visited. Others fumble and appear much worse than normal. My advice is — unless you are in that classroom enough for the teacher to become comfortable with your presence, you are just wasting your time and creating the illusion of evaluation.

Saying "evaluation" to teachers is too often like flinging a racial slur in the ghetto. With many individuals it is a call to do battle. The reason for this angry response is the burdensome history of imprecision and unfairness that has surrounded teacher evaluation.

Let me offer some workable suggestions to enable teacher evaluation to take place in the best and fairest climate possible.

Testing Teachers
Let's make the following improvements:
1) Let's be highly specific about what composes teacher proficiency.
2) Let's put the incentives for achieving proficiency up front.
3) Let's offer a feedback mechanism, including coaching as needed, to help teachers identify opportunity for growth.
4) Let's reward teachers and schools for their collective achievements.

Classroom Proficiencies To Be Evaluated
The classroom proficiencies to be evaluated could be grouped into manageable units such as classroom questioning skills, counseling skills, classroom management skills, and lesson delivery skills such as deductive and inductive lessons.

1) **Classroom Questions:** While observing the teacher in the classroom, the observer would focus on whether or not the teacher has comfortably internalized classroom questioning skills to a 90 percent execution level. Mastery would include Memory, Comprehension, Creative, and Evaluation questioning modes. Comprehension, Creative, and Evaluation questions should exceed memory-level questions in frequency of use. Evaluation of classroom questions would include an appraisal of Clarity, Pause Time, Probes and Responses to student answers.

   The judges would debrief at the end of a 40-minute live or videotaped presentation, praising positive areas of the teacher's performance and suggesting areas for improvement.
2) **Counseling:** Counseling would be judged in two 20-minute simulations, one involving a parent and one involving a student. The role plays would be selected from a published list of 20 case studies. During the role play the expert-observer would evaluate the teacher's fluidity, flexibility, and expertise in delivering an appropriate skill or strategy for each situation.

3) **Deductive Lesson Skills:** This proficiency might parallel some of Madeline Hunter's recommendations, including the presentation of a "compelling why" and a lesson limit of seven bits of new information. The lesson material should be taught three different ways: Kinesthetically, Visually, and Auditorily. The material should be explained Abstractly, Concretely, Globally, and Sequentially, with accompanying verb rotations, with a memory hook enabling the information to be retained in the long-term memory, and with an effective mix of activities that help internalization.

4) **Inductive Lesson Skills:** This proficiency refers to the skills of the teacher in creating instances (experiences) from which students can achieve generalizations (outcomes, conclusions). These generalizations are then used to create an action plan (synthesis). There are varieties of methodologies and verbal skills that teachers use to promote student thinking.

5) **Classroom Management Proficiency:** The classroom management proficiency would include these non curricular aspects of teaching: Positive Phrasing, Enthusiasm, Clarity, Congruence, Teacher Positioning, Student Tactical Emplacement, Transitional Timing, Momentum Strategies, Nonconfrontation Strategies, Team-building Strategies, Use of a Reward/Penalty System, and Classroom Organization.

The classroom management proficiency could be demonstrated both in the classroom and through a 30-minute "what if" format involving hypothetical situations. "What if Judy was daydreaming? How would you bring her attention back to the task at hand?"

A sixth possible set of proficiencies, which I will call the Knowledge Proficiencies, would be knowledge of from 1,000 to 10,000 published education facts which every practicing teacher should know. A specific example of such a fact might be age level and brain growth of students and the bearing on student learning.

These facts should be published with the sample questions from ten sample tests. What we expect teachers to know should be clearly spelled out. A justification, a "compelling why" for the 10,000 facts relating to the practice of classroom teaching, should be established in advance. In short, the facts should be useful.

Ten Suggestions To Improve the Evaluation Process

Suggestion 1: The standard for execution of the proficiency will be 90% accuracy.

Suggestion 2: The teaching process should be evaluated through the use of videotapes of lessons. "We need video cameras — and funds to pay experts to analyze teaching, just as coaches analyze the performances of athletes." A teacher can set up two cameras in the classroom — one covering the teacher from the rear of the room and one at the side, covering the students. Then the tapes can be sent to experts for evaluation.

The expert can write comments keyed to the counter on the recorder or VCR, such as, "Notice at 375 a student walks in late. You reprimand him. Notice you lost three minutes in the tardiness discussion. Observe how the class body language turns negative as the discussion progresses. A suggestion: write down his name and continue the lesson without interrupting the momentum. Later, ask the student to stay after class."

Suggestion 3: The teaching process should be broken down into parts and each part evaluated sequentially.

Suggestion 4: There should be classifications of desired proficiencies and cash awards for achieving these proficiencies. Of course, the awards should be made in agreement with the collective bargaining unit. An award could be anything from a salary credit recognition for a proficiency certificate equal on the salary schedule to a Master's degree or cash for the six areas listed, or both.

Suggestion 5: The judges should be highly regarded experts, able to certify the teacher for receipt of a cash award. The judges should be highly trained to ensure interrater reliability. Such training ensures that an understanding of a definition for good teaching is present in the evaluation process. "Evaluations must be made by several persons working with specific multifaceted and clearly articulated guidelines."[84] PLS estimates that it requires 300 hours of training for an evaluater to have interrater reliability.

Suggestion 6: Areas in which the teacher needs to improve should be communicated to the teacher in clear, concise, positively phrased language that defines exactly how improvement can best be achieved.

Suggestion 7: The teacher should be allowed to request four separate observations of his or her execution of the four proficiency groupings. This would parallel the execution of forehand, backhand, serve, and volley skills in tennis, or be analogous to mastering the drive, long game, chipping game, and putting skills in golf.

Suggestion 8: The teacher will know, will have practiced, and will have been trained in the proficiency to be evaluated.

Let me underscore that the evaluation of skills is not evaluation of vision, strategy, or tactics, nor is it evaluation of judgment about which reasonable people can differ. Judging skills of a musician is independent of the musician's recital choice of music.

Suggestion 9: The teacher will have been perfecting the proficiency for several months or years.

Suggestion 10: Coaching will have been available to the teacher during the preparation period.

Career Ladders Arising From Evaluation

I envision a career ladder with four levels. If Level I is the entry level, Level III is the top of the career ladder. The goal is to move from Level I to Level III. Level III teachers would be the ones most often referred to as Master Teachers under other plans. These teachers are characterized by their fluidity in moving between teaching protocols.

A Level IV teacher is the Teacher Educator/Evaluator, a position to be held by a few carefully selected and trained successful Level III teachers. California SB813 has provided for something of this sort by decreeing that a few first-rate teachers are to be tapped as mentors for their peers and are to receive a yearly bonus of $4,000 each.

Training hundreds of mentors in California has made it clear to me that the selection process is a hodgepodge of good guesses. We have had dozens of teachers admit they have no idea why they were chosen. Spending money without precisely implemented criteria proves the unsettled state of evaluation. When no apparent criteria are used there is room for "patronage" and "favoritism" charges. In California, where teachers apply for consideration, many "best" teachers do not apply because being awarded $4,000 isn't worth the sniping remarks of colleagues. This is why criteria and expert, independent evaluation must be implemented.

Level I

A Level I teacher is still developing skills in delivering proficiencies, in doing more than one thing at a time, each with precision and finesse. Usually, a Level I teacher is a beginning teacher. Paul R. Burden, who identifies three stages of professional growth in his paper "Professional Development as a Stressor," speaks of Stage I — the first year of a teacher's experience — this way:

> Teachers in Stage I, the survival stage, were uncertain and confused about many aspects of the job. They didn't feel confident and were not certain how the situation would improve. They often were not sure how to deal with certain problems, were frustrated, and wondered if they were "measuring up." They also expressed the need to feel confident, effective, and competent in the first year but apparently did not achieve these feelings....Much of their uncertainty in the survival stage resulted from their feelings of inadequacy in:
>   1) maintaining classroom control,
>   2) teaching the subject,
>   3) improving their teaching skills.
> The teachers' feelings of stress, therefore, were primarily a result of concerns about their job skills, knowledge, and behavior.[85]

Level II

Our Level II teacher has honed each skill and is still concentrating on being able to employ all the skills in a multiple concentration. Burden defines his Stage II — roughly analogous to our Level II teachers — this way:

> Teachers in Stage II, the adjustment stage, were gaining confidence and were more comfortable with what they were doing, with the subject matter, and with the teaching techniques they were using. The teachers were more relaxed and sure of themselves but still didn't feel capable of handling any situation which might arise. . .Teachers at Stage II, the adjustment stage, have learned from their first year experiences and have acquired job skills and information in a number of areas. They are more able to look at their needs more objectively and seek out assistance. [86]

Burden says of Stage II teachers, "...the teachers started to see the complexities in the children and sought new teaching techniques to meet the wider range of needs they were beginning to perceive. Their feelings of stress at this stage often centered on their adequacy in varying their instruction and meeting the wide range of student needs."[87]

Level III

Level III teachers are far more sensitive than others in their multiple concentration ability and in discerning the critical stimuli in their environment and acting on such stimuli smoothly and accurately. Level III teachers can make complex decisions with confidence. They can adroitly regain their composure if they stumble.

As Burden says of his Stage III teacher,

"By this mature stage, the teachers had become skilled in a variety of techniques and continually tried additional techniques to increase their competence, to passively accept change, and to keep teaching interesting for themselves. The teachers focused on their own personal improvement and challenge."[88]

Positiveness is a large part of the Level III teacher's mastery of the craft. They maintain warm eye contact with students, closing the distance between them and personalizing the message.

Level III teachers also handle disruptions and critical incidents smoothly. They understand, as B.O. Smith of the University of South Florida puts it, that "teachers who maintain instructional momentum have fewer disruptions than teachers who allow the momentum to drag or die."[89]

Level III teachers almost never interrupt the momentum of a classroom lesson to deal with classroom incidents. The most overt action they might take would be to write the offending student's name on a note pad. A class rule might be that the student would have to meet the teacher after class. A check mark after the name might mean 15 minutes of detention, etc. While different Level III teachers might handle misbehavior differently, each Level III teacher has the ability to continue the lesson smoothly and without interruption.

Comparison: I versus II versus III

Level II teachers can ask their students a question, observe the reaction of the entire class, and allow a reasonable pause time. However, a Level III teacher does all that and also knows that more complex questions require more pause time. Level III teachers have an immediately accessible memory bank to tell them which students are best at answering which kinds of questions. They track student answers so that all students can give good answers three out of four times, giving everyone a sense of success.

By contrast, the Level II teacher can only use one skill at a time. The Level II teacher knows how to respond to correct, incorrect, or incomplete answers. The Level III teacher will know when to go on, continuing to question the same student, probing more deeply for the correct or fuller answer or calling on another student to continue the answer. The Level III teacher handles questioning so smoothly and deftly that all the students have a feeling of success.

By contrast, the Level II teacher is awkward at reading the students and reveals this awkwardness in flustered vocal tone changes. "A number of studies have consistently shown that skill in verbal discourse can contribute significantly to student achievement."[90]

The Level III teacher moves easily from a question skill to a reading think time skill, to handling a disruption, to any other skill in the teaching repertoire. Basically, what separates a Level III teacher from a Level II teacher is the former's ability to make a smooth transition from one skill proficiency to another and to apply two or more skills at the same time. An example is moving in closer to one student who is off-task while asking another student a clearly framed question.

As Joan L. Fogarty and others at Pittsburgh University confirmed, in relation to our comparisons of Level I versus Level III teachers:

> Experienced teachers used twice as many kinds of instructional actions and considered a greater variety of goals while exhibiting more complex associations between cue and action categories. Novices were less likely to incorporate spontaneous student input related to lesson content and attended to cues from individual students rather than cues from the group as a whole.[91]

The only person who should evaluate teachers for continuation or salary upgrade is a proven Level III teacher. The bind is, there are few educators who know the 160 plus skill and performance patterns in the same action sense that an Olympic skating judge knows a skater's moves.

Rewards for Superior Teachers

An enlightened rewards system has potential group dynamics advantages. First, each teacher who earns a cash award could also garner an additional cash award for all teachers in the building, because of the success of one individual teacher in achieving a certain proficiency level. This would encourage both individual and group achievement and place positive pressure on each individual to take part.

This group dynamic would encourage teachers to prep and coach each other, and it would especially encourage winners to help others to achieve the same goal. Merit raises should not be reserved for a few superior teachers but must reward all who help achieve a specific objective.

This operation reinforces the need for experts independent of the system. A referee in a sporting event would be asking for trouble if he was evaluating his own players.

After achieving an understanding of the school goals in terms of effective school research, a superior evaluation could earn a pool of money to be divided among schools in a district as a reward for a positive school climate. When one school is awarded $200 per teacher and another school is awarded $900, the $900 school celebrates its apparent success and the $200 per teacher school evaluates its internal dynamics and plans for improvement for the following year.

Recognized Problems of Evaluation

Any reward system will only work if the judge is an established "educators' educator"; that is, the judges must have peer respect as outstanding colleagues and teachers. Judges must be highly trained for consistent reliability. There should be a quality control system to check the integrity of the judges' ratings in the field. Every judge must be at least a proven Level III.

The inherent problem with evaluation and documentation is whether or not the evaluator and documentor is sophisticated and proficient enough to evaluate what he sees, hears, and feels. An evaluator is both judge and diplomat, if successful. There is an immense backlog of resistance to be dealt with — from teacher doubt through outright anger at the evaluation process.

"Evaluation frequently arouses fear and activates defensiveness on the part of teachers."[92] "Teachers are justified in demanding that the evaluators be highly competent and well-trained, especially when judgments about a teacher's worth or merit are being made."[93]

Unless teachers can feel completely confident that the evaluation will be unbiased and professional, their cooperation is unlikely. Neal Nickerson declared that "the objectivity of the person determining merit is always suspect"[94] and Gary Adkins determined that "the factor common to groups opposed to teacher merit pay is the fear of unfair evaluation criteria."[95] Teachers themselves, via their teacher organizations, should have a say in establishing who shall judge.

Benefits of a Fair Evaluation System

There is no question that there are some vastly inferior teachers at the top of their salary scales who are earning twice the money of superior teachers at the bottom of the salary scale. That is grossly unfair, and it's happening in every school district in every city in every state and province across the land. That is why I favor proficiency pay over the existing seniority and hours system. Merit pay programs are based on the simple idea that educators should be paid what they are worth. Unfortunately, the criteria and the experts should have been proved first.

Establishing the evaluation rewards and techniques discussed in this chapter might well prove to be the positive revisionist force that teachers desire and that the public indicates, in poll after poll, that it desires. This sort of systematic method of reviewing a teacher's performance in the classroom is a realistic plan to improve both teacher performance and morale. It deserves careful consideration.

B.O. Smith, considering the most recent public outcry for educational reform, wrote:

> Why have all these complaints, all these proposals for school improvement, and all these reform efforts of each generation led to further complaints and further efforts by the next generation? I do not know the answer for certain, but I can speculate. Could the answer be that we really do not know whether the schools are better or worse and that this uncertainty periodically spills over into a national seizure of anxiety? Could it be that we have never reconciled ourselves to mass education and that we really do not want to cope with what it means?

Could it be that the education establishment is so loosely jointed and so massive that no nationwide change can be sustained? Could the answer be that the reformers fly by the seats of their pants, knowing neither what changes to make nor how to make them? Could it be that the profession has been, and continues to be, poorly prepared, locked into a static system of professional immobility and denied ample return on investment in preparation? Could the answer be that the knowledge base for school improvement is ignored — the existing knowledge not used nor its continued development supported? It is unlikely that any one of these potential answers is sufficient in itself. But perhaps there is some truth in all of them.[96]

I have spent almost two decades working with literally thousands of experienced, respected, competent professionals who teach in the United States and Canada. For 20 years I have been informed by extensive research, and development within our organization and that done by others. At Performance Learning Systems we have focused on exploring the profession of the much maligned and long-neglected classroom teacher. They are the people who really run education and have the awesome responsibility of making it work in today's schools.

The profession needs more of this sort of no-nonsense, real-world investigation. We now know what makes good teachers tick from firsthand interaction and observation. We also feel we do know what changes to make and how to make them, based on research and experience in the field.

Once we train specific skills, we have something concrete to evaluate. That seemingly small difference can make a massive contribution to improving education. To create champion teachers, they must be treated like champions. They must be made to know that they are an important part of a winning organization.

Chapter 14   It's Working in the Real World

"Man who say it cannot be done should not interrupt man doing it."—Chinese Proverb

---

*T*he methods, the skills, the strategies I've been talking about are in use, producing award-winning staff development plans, better teachers and students who are more likely to find a place in the rapidly changing world that awaits them.

This chapter was written so readers could appreciate the variety of teacher development programs as they plan their own programs. In some cases the district adopts or creates a plan to improve teaching skills. Or, a college or university department of education incorporates classroom skills into a Master's degree program. Sometimes the development program is supported and presented by the teacher organization. Often two or three of these groups work cooperatively to develop a program.

The vital difference between analysis and synthesis is courage. It's one thing to talk a good game and another to play a good game.

Real courage is required to move from the research to action. In the following case studies, real people have taken real risks and have experienced the hardships of pioneering some notions about teacher development. This is how far they have come and where they are going. Here classroom skills training is making a real difference in education. The case studies were chosen for their diversity.

Case Study #1: California
Sweetwater School District

LOCATION: Southern California, close to the Mexican border.
No. of SCHOOLS IN DISTRICT: 23
No. of TEACHERS IN DISTRICT: 1,200
STUDENT POPULATION: 25,000

PROFESSIONAL TRAINING STAFF: 100
TEACHERS TRAINED: 400 since 1984
COURSE CYCLE: Project T.E.A.C.H., P.R.I.D.E., TEACHING through LEARNING CHANNELS — repeats every third semester. At the writing of this book, Sheridan Barker is in charge of the development program.
UNUSUALS: California's largest secondary school district, 69.2% Hispanic student body. Superintendent Anthony Trujillo wanted a development plan that would bring students who have dropped out back into the system, while setting high standards for the district and helping teachers to raise their expectations. The Sweetwater teacher development plan was selected as one of nine exemplary programs in the country by the American Association of School Administrators.
REWARDS: Voluntary program, provides teachers with salary barrier credit. Voluntary training has been so successful, the district is making it required — on the advice of teachers already trained.
COMMENTS: Sheridan Barker, Staff Development Director: "If we can create an environment in the school system that says 'It's okay to grow, it's okay to experiment, and we'll support you in the process,' then we'll have teachers who continue to grow. And in the long run we'll have kids who will really benefit from this development process. The risks are simply too great to allow our teachers to spend three years, or ten years, figuring out how to be good teachers. We can't risk ten years of students. We want to give every student in our system the opportunity to choose to go on to higher education. We are trying to provide students with a high quality education so that when they leave school they will have choices. In Sweetwater we're beginning to make a difference. We're already seeing dramatic upward changes in our testing scores, in our student achievement and in the number of students enrolling in college."[97]

Case Study #2: New Jersey
Kinnelon School District

LOCATION: Morris County, New Jersey.
No. of SCHOOLS IN DISTRICT: 2 elementary, 1 middle, 1 high school
No. of TEACHERS IN DISTRICT: 200
STUDENT POPULATION: 1,400
PROFESSIONAL TRAINING STAFF: 1

TEACHERS TRAINED: 70 since 1984
COURSE CYCLE: Project T.E.A.C.H., P.R.I.D.E., TEACHING through LEARNING CHANNELS, COACHING TEACHERS to HIGHER LEVELS of EFFECTIVENESS.
REWARDS: 95% of participation is voluntary. District pays for training.
COMMENTS: Training takes place after school hours.

Case Study #3: Iowa
Drake University

LOCATION: Teachers are trained off campus in districts throughout the state of Iowa.
PROFESSIONAL TRAINING STAFF: 40
No. of TEACHERS IN THE STATE: 33,000
TEACHERS TRAINED: 10,000 in past five years
COURSE CYCLE: Project T.E.A.C.H., P.R.I.D.E., TEACHING through LEARNING CHANNELS, Patterns for I.D.E.A.S.
UNUSUALS: Master's degree program created by Drake in cooperation with the Iowa State Education Association was commended publicly by Mary Hatwood Futrell, National Education Association President.
REWARDS: Training is voluntary, taken toward Master's degree. Teachers pay their own way.
COMMENTS: Dr. Charles S. Greenwood, Assistant Dean of the College of Education: "We urge teachers to select skills training courses as electives in one Master's program. In a second Master's degree program we *require* teachers to take those courses. They are required because they are the best courses available to give teachers the classroom skills they need to be successful."

Here is another example of an instituion of higher learning deciding to include classroom skills in its education curriculum.

Case Study #4: Ontario
Ontario Public School Teachers' Federation

LOCATION: Toronto, Ontario, Canada
PROFESSIONAL TRAINING STAFF: 75:
TEACHERS TRAINED: 14,000 since 1976
COURSE CYCLE: Project T.E.A.C.H., P.R.I.D.E., TEACHING through LEARNING CHANNEL, Patterns for I.D.E.A.S.,

COACHING TEACHERS to HIGHER LEVELS of EFFECTIVENESS.
UNUSUALS: In addition to training teachers, the Federation trains principals to train other principals and vice principals in 27 hours of coaching instruction. Boards purchase Thursday evenings and full-day Friday instruction (3 times) through the Federation. More than 300 educators in pivotal positions have taken this instruction. The result is a greater sensitivity by principals to be concrete and specific.

REWARDS: Teachers take the training for salary barrier credit.

COMMENTS: J. W. Atkinson, Federation Professional Development Director: "The courses are practical, they're hands-on. The materials that are presented are usable immediately. The overwhelming success of these programs lies in their practical application to the classroom. What they learn in these courses allows teachers to spend more time teaching and less time managing their classes. By giving them better classroom management techniques, the training makes them better able to get on with the real job of teaching youngsters."

Case Study #5: New York
Rochester Peer Assistance Review Program

LOCATION: Upstate New York
No. of SCHOOLS IN DISTRICT: 30
PROFESSIONAL TRAINING STAFF: 22 full-time mentors
TEACHERS TRAINED: 150 intern teachers since 1986
UNUSUALS: Training is administered through the New York State United Teachers Effective Teaching program which has trained 15,000 teachers cooperatively with Long Island University.

REWARDS: Mentors spend their time helping improve the practical classroom teaching skills of first-year teachers.

COMMENTS: Adam Urbanski, President of the Rochester Teachers Association: "After the startup phase, the mentors became half-time teachers again, with release time to work with the new teachers. We believe that teachers who coach other teachers should, themselves, remain practitioners. Schools will be restructured in Rochester and throughout the country. You cannot unring the bell of reform and the raised aspirations of teachers."

Districts are working in cooperation with universities to provide training that earns teachers higher education credit.

Case Study #6: Florida
Pasco County School District

LOCATION: Suburban Tampa.
No. of SCHOOLS IN DISTRICT: 37
No. of TEACHERS IN DISTRICT: 1,500
STUDENT POPULATION: 30,300
PROFESSIONAL TRAINING STAFF: 100
TEACHERS TRAINED: 600 since 1985
COURSE CYCLE: Project T.E.A.C.H., P.R.I.D.E., TEACHING through LEARNING CHANNELS.
REWARDS: Training is voluntary, district pays costs. Higher education credit is available through the University of South Florida.
COMMENTS: Dr. Joyce Swarzman, University of South Florida: "The best possible people should be in our schools. To keep these quality people in education, identify them, then make them feel special. Third, give them a professional attitude that leads to a commitment to education."[98]

Case Study #7: Florida
Alachua County School District

LOCATION: Gainesville
No. of SCHOOLS IN DISTRICT: 32
No. of TEACHERS IN DISTRICT: 1,500
STUDENT POPULATION: 22,580
PROFESSIONAL TRAINING STAFF: 100
TEACHERS TRAINED: 750 1986-87
COURSE CYCLE: Project T.E.A.C.H., P.R.I.D.E., TEACHING through LEARNING CHANNELS.
UNUSUALS: All principals in the district have been trained in COACHING TEACHERS to HIGHER LEVELS of EFFECTIVENESS. That training is now being extended to assistant principals and superintendents.
REWARDS: Training is voluntary and paid for by the district. Graduate credit is available through the University of Florida.
COMMENTS: Fay Cake, Director of Staff Development: "Teachers I recognize as already being excellent teachers are reporting high increases in their teaching effectiveness. It looks like the training is helping our good teachers get even better."

In some cases, districts are joining together to provide the needed training.

Case Study #8: Illinois
Wabash and Ohio Valley Special Education District

LOCATION: In nine rural Illinois counties a consortium of small school districts provides training to their teachers.
No. of DISTRICTS: 24
No. of SCHOOLS: 110
STUDENT POPULATION: 24,000
PROFESSIONAL TRAINING STAFF: 15
TEACHERS TRAINED: 300 since 1986
COURSE CYCLE: Project T.E.A.C.H., P.R.I.D.E., TEACHING through LEARNING CHANNELS.
UNUSUALS: Both school administrators and teachers are receiving classroom skills training.
REWARDS: The teachers who have been trained, and their school administrators, have a common language to discuss the ongoing development of specific teaching skills.
COMMENTS: Joseph Glassford, Director of the Wabash and Ohio Valley Special Education District: "The skills training produced a request from the participating administrators for instruction in coaching skills, so they can continue to support teacher growth."

A Common Thread

All of these programs have several things in common. They all are acts of courage, wherein districts, colleges and universities, or teacher organizations, recognize that teachers need and want to have the classroom skills that will make them successful. They have taken a forceful stride toward the improvements we all want to see in education.

In all of these cases, Performance Learning Systems designed the courses, provides the training of instructors, provides one or two meetings for instructors per year, and provides a toll-free 800 telephone line for instant telephone coaching. Evaluations of the training are tabulated and that feedback is given to instructors. Instructors who get low evaluations are either coached to improve or released. A monthly newsletter keeps instructors abreast of training techniques. More than half of PLS instructors nationwide are in a coaching network. Instructors are chosen through a rigorous process of selection from the top 5% of the teaching force.

These are models we have been working with for up to 15 years. What readers will not see here are the formidable challenges that PLS and its sponsors have faced over the years in institutionalizing these programs. Nor will the energy be obvious that was required to secure the support and funding.

The case histories in this chapter are good examples of the new awareness educators are showing toward on-the-job training of teachers. A sense of responsibility for providing skills and feedback to new and veteran teachers is growing in the districts. Administrators are accepting the responsibility of continuing teacher education in the classroom skills that facilitate learning.

To be successful, teacher training must have support. The board of education—the funding agency—must support the effort. Administrators must help to make the plan successful and teacher organizations must add their positive efforts. To get all these groups marching in the right direction is a tremendous feat. The degree to which the districts have accomplished this feat is a direct measure of the success of their teacher training programs.

Those who succeed are enlightened educators who have discovered that training performing artists goes far beyond the football team and school band.

Chapter 15

In Conclusion: Through the Window

"Parties who want milk should not seat themselves on a stool in the middle of a field in hope that the cow will back up to them."—Elbert Hubbard

*L*et me say again what I said to begin this book.

We have before us right now the opportunity to change and vastly improve the quality of the education our children will receive.

The Carnegie Report, <u>A Nation Prepared: Teachers for the 21st Century</u>, summarizes the current and future education situation with these cutting words:

> America's ability to compete in world markets is eroding. The productivity growth of our competitors out distances our own. The capacity of our economy to provide a high standard of living for all our people is increasingly in doubt. As jobs requiring little skill are automated or go offshore, and demand increases for the highly skilled, the pool of educated and skilled people grows smaller and the backwater of the unemployable rises. Large numbers of American children are in limbo — ignorant of the past and unprepared for the future. Many are dropping out — not just out of school but out of productive society.[99]

The high school dropout rate has climbed toward 30% from a relatively constant dropout rate of 20% over the last decade. In some cities 50% of all high school students drop out before graduation.[100]

We are seeing a scramble to fund plans that will turn the dropout situation around. In this planning, one key concept must be kept firmly in mind: curriculum doesn't teach students, teachers do.

If there is one message more important than any other in today's clamor for improvement in educating teachers, it is that we are violating our own education research. We must follow the research on the internalization of behavior, from skill definition to incentives for accomplishing goals. Teachers have for too long been given a vague job description, have been required to internalize practices without training, and have had feedback and evaluations based on vague sets of criteria that they suspect are tainted with favoritism and patronage.

At this point in time, let's make sure that calls for education reform end with neither the whimper nor the bang of T.S. Eliot's famous poem.

The magic of the great teacher lies in the performance. The great teacher, like the great magician, or a champion athlete, or an award-winning artist, can only be produced through the practice and coaching of fundamental skills.

Teaching is a complex tapestry integrating knowledge, skill, talent, and love for the students and the profession. We need to show teachers and administrators how to weave these threads into successful skill and performance patterns that will produce great teachers and better student learning.

The Five-Year Window

We are in a five-year window of time, 1988 to 1993, when the vast majority of teachers and teacher educators will be retiring, to be replaced by new teachers. Now is the time when implementation of reform measures will adversely affect the smallest number of people.

These few critical years, used wisely, can enable us to effect the changes that will produce capable, educated adults whose chances of success and meaningful contribution to society have been greatly enhanced by our timely action.

This window of opportunity can significantly improve teacher education. At this crucial time a sense of responsibility to future generations of students, and the quality of their education, must guide us. Meaningful reform must be implemented.

To do what must be done for education, we have to tackle this list of priorities:

1) **All teachers must master the generic teaching skills**.
2) **Teacher educators must model effective teaching practices.**

3) **All licensed school district personnel, including administrators, should be involved in teacher development programs.** With a common knowledge of teaching skills, and a common language, administrators can support and positively evaluate teacher progress.

4) **Teacher training must take place in the workplace, with coaching and feedback.** Instead of lectures, reading, and paper writing, teachers must be trained in a safe environment where helpfulness is the standard.

5) **Incentive systems for teachers must be revamped to provide rewards for training and internalization of what was trained.** Emphasis must be shifted from solely acquiring knowledge to the inclusion of the "hows" of teaching.

In Summary

Earlier in this book we saw how incentives were seen in the 1950s and the 1960s as a means of improving teaching. But, the joke was on all of us — teachers, administrators, and parents. All the advanced knowledge-oriented courses did was create the illusion that more courses produced a better teacher. They didn't teach the performing art of teaching.

We at Performance Learning Systems practice what we preach. Every aspect of the suggestions we make, we *use* ourselves with our own team of personnel. Morale and mission are sky-high because the research on individual and organization effectiveness is correct. Putting the research into use is the best decision we as a group have ever made. Leadership starts by modeling the message of helping every team member be everything they can be. We are extra sensitive to individual differences, attributes, and yearnings.

We notice that the education community is caught by analysis paralysis and power gridlock. We encourage educators to think about their vision, yearnings, and attributes ...and *do something.* In the end it is what we make happen that is the best measure of what we believe.

And, we have a windfall — the difference between starting and retiring salaries as senior teachers retire.

A fresh concept — the teacher as a performing artist — will help us to provide the skill and performance patterns training our teachers need. Coupled with coaching — long-term positive help and reinforcement — this concept can, and is, making our classrooms better places of learning. The more than 100 specific skills observed in great teachers can be internalized by every teacher. We can provide a common language for teaching staffs and offer an established basis for evaluating teacher performance in concrete specific ways that are fair.

Conclusion I

Talent includes attribute identification and skill/ knowledge training, plus coaching. Quality relationships include a safe environment and celebration of success. Expectations include a clear vision and mission statement with attributes that fit to the organization. Therefore, talent times relationships, plus expectations equals optimum success.

The model of how to train teachers is the best model to educate students. We find the education community, including how we teach students, grossly out of sync in practice with researched conclusions. Allow educators to feel the power of attribute development and they will use it.

Conclusion II

The most efficient internalization for all people in all subjects is to train skills for use in a typical scenario. When success is achieved, knowledge (research) becomes internalized and attitudes change. Again, the education community, including students, is out of sync with its own research.

Conclusion III

Educators at all levels have different visions, mission statements and attributes. Educators vary in their motivation depending on the amount of direct leadership and control placed on them. The "system" is out of sync with its own research. Giving power is gaining power. The model of the future is focusing on the attitudes, expectations and visions of better educators at all levels, fitting the "system" to them.

Conclusion IV

The future is with synthesis research. Some college courses, as research, learning theory, statistics, test and measurements, should be shaped into "active courses" where 200 to 500 teachers in 10 to 20 classes compare teaching strategies and lesson formats, feeding the results into computers to get a professionally written analysis in a common language.

Conclusion V

Coaching by an expert is the most effective internalization medium. Staff development is a cost-effective way for an educator to internalize beginning patterns of performance. Both must occur in the workplace in a safe environment.

Conclusion VI

The test of the competence of evaluators or coaches is, "Can the evaluator (or coach) tell the educator in cause and effect terms what skill and strategy options worked and might have worked better in the 'live' classroom?" And, "Does the evaluator (or coach) have the teaching competence to demonstrate the performance move by move?"

We have a limited time to recognize and implement the excellent tools that exist to remake teacher training in a way that will cost less and give us more in the long run.

The five-year window closes in less than five years.

What society, politicians, parents, administrators, and educators do during this important time in history will affect the quality of learning for the next hundred years. Education will either go through the five-year window to provide capable, effective teachers for our children. . .or education may well be swept out the back door like a burned-out light bulb.

The reader has some very basic decisions to make. Will you be an informed participant in the events that shape the future of education? Will you influence others to join the events? Will you add your voice to the call for Champion Teachers to provide a world class education for our young people?

The choice is yours.

Footnotes

1. The Condition of Education. National Center for Education Statistics. July 19, 1985.

2. Tomorrow's Teachers: A Report of The Holmes Group. East Lansing, MI. April, 1986, p. 3.

3. Ibid., p. 19.

4. Ibid., p. 64.

5. Ibid., p. 49.

6. Ibid., p. 52.

7. Ibid., p. 53.

8. Ibid., p. 54.

9. Ibid., p. 59

10. Ibid., p. 59.

11. Gage, N.L. "What Do We Know About Teaching Effectiveness?" Phi Delta Kappan, October, 1984, p. 92.

12. Cohen, David K. "Teaching Practice from the Practitioner's Perspective." Huron Institute, Cambridge, Massachusetts, April, 1983: ERIC ED 237 491.

13 Ibid.

14. Hunter, Madeline, and Doug Russell. "Critical Attributes of a Staff Development Program to Increase Instructional Effectiveness," p. 1. University of California at Los Angeles.

15. Nottingham, Marv. "Teacher Appraisal for Career Ladders." Idaho Teacher Excellence Program 1985: ERIC ED 257 215.

16. Ishler, Peggy. "Upgrading Education Means Upgrading the Teacher Evaluation System: Merging Evaluation Information and Effective Teaching Research — an Inservice Approach." Bowling Green SU, Ohio. Paper presented at the Annual Meeting of the Association of Teacher Educators. Feb., 1984: ERIC ED 241 486.

17. Wood, Fred H. "Mining Good Staff Development Ideas in Business." NCR Training Program, Dayton, Ohio, 1983.

18. Hunter, Madeline, and Doug Russell. "Critical Attributes of a Staff Development Program to Increase Instructional Effectiveness."

19. Dodd, Anne Wescott, and Eileen Rosenbaum. "Learning Communities for Curriculum and Staff Development." Phi Delta Kappan, Jan., 1986 67(5), 380-385.

20. Tomorrow's Teachers: A Report of the Holmes Group, p. 15.

21. Ibid., p. 16.

22. Shanker, Albert. "The Making of a Profession." Speech delivered to the Representative Assembly of New York State United Teachers, April 27, 1985, reprinted in American Educator, Fall, 1985 9(3), 10-17, 46.

23. Ibid.

24. Tomorrow's Teachers: A Report of The Holmes Group, p. 61.

25. Shanker, Albert. "The Making of a Profession."

26. "Raise Status of Teaching, Colleges Told." Education Week. November 5, 1986. p.7.

27. "President of Harvard Urges Education School Revival." Education Week, April 29, 1987.

28. Marso and Pigge, "Differences Between Self-Perceived Job Expectations and Job Realities of Beginning Teachers." Journal of Teacher Education, November- December, 1987.

29. Los Angeles Times, March 16, 1988.

30. "President of Harvard Urges Education School Revival." Education Week, April 29, 1987.

31. Cohen, David K., "Teaching Practice from the Practitioners Perspective." Huron Institute, Cambridge, Massachusetts, April, 1983: ERIC ED 237 491 p.5.

32. A Nation Prepared: Teachers for the 21st Century, Carnegie Forum on Education and the Economy. Report of the Task Force on Teaching as a Profession. May, 1986.

33. Wood, Fred H. "Mining Good Staff Development Ideas in Business." NCR Training Program, Dayton, Ohio, 1983.

34. Ibid.

35. Anderson, W.S., quoted in Fred H. Wood's "Mining Good Staff Development Ideas in Business."

36. Wood, Fred H. "Mining Good Staff Development Ideas in Business."

37. Ibid.

38. Ibid.

39. Levin, Henry M. Cost-Effectiveness: A Primer Beverly Hills, Calif.: Sage, 1983, p. 15.

40. Annual Back to School Forecast, U.S. Department of Education Center for Statistics, 1986.

41. Harris, Karen R. and others. "The Relationship Between Pupil Control Ideology, Self Concept and Teacher Personality: Dimensions of Teacher Effectiveness." Boston, Massachusetts, May, 1982: ERIC ED 216 412.

42. Gage, N.L. "What Do We Know About Teaching Effectiveness?" Phi Delta Kappan, October, 1984.

43. McNergney, Robert and Lyn Satterstrom. "Teacher Characteristics and Teacher Performance." UMI, January, 1984: ERIC ED 296 206.

44. Rubin, Louis. "The Artist Teacher." Illinois School Research and Development, Fall, 1981 18(1), 1-7.

45. Cuban, Larry. "School Reform by Remote Control: SB813 in California." Phi Delta Kappan, November, 1984, 213-215.

46. Ibid.

47. Hunter, Madeline, and Doug Russell. "Critical Attributes of a Staff Development Program to Increase Instructional Effectiveness." University of California at Los Angeles.

48. Cohen, David K. "Teaching Practice from the Practitioner's Perspective." Huron Institute, Cambridge, Massachusetts, April, 1983: ERIC ED 237 491.

49. Rubin, Louis. "The Artist Teacher."

50. Gage, N.L. "What Do We Know About Teaching Effectiveness?"

51. Cohen, David K. "Teaching Practice from the Practitioner's Perspective."

52. Fast, Julius. Body Language. New York: M. Evans and Company, Inc., 1970.

53. Denton, Jon J. and others. "Characteristics of Student Teachers and Cognitive Attainment of their Learners." Paper prepared for the Annual Meeting of the Association of Teacher Educators. Texas A&M, February, 1981.

54. Defino, Maria E. and Heather Carter. "Changing Teacher Practices: Proceedings of a National Conference." Texas University, Austin, Texas, February, 1982: ERIC ED 223 582.

55. Edwards, Sara. "Changing Teacher Practices: A Synthesis of Relevant Research." Texas Univ., Austin, September, 1981: ERIC ED 223 566.

56. Gillett, Max and Meredith Gail. "The Effects of Teacher Enthusiasm on the At-Task Behavior of Students in Elementary Grades." Australia, 1980: ERIC ED 216 412.

57. "Pointers for Teachers" from List of Qualified Teachers and School Officers for Wayne County, Michigan, 1900-1901, Phi Delta Kappan, February, 1986, Vol. 67, No. 6.

58. Berliner, David C. "On the Expert Teacher," Educational Leadership, October, 1986.

59. Cohen, David K. "Teaching Practice from the Practitioner's Perspective." Huron Institute, Cambridge, Massachusetts, April, 1983: ERIC ED 237 491.

60. Ibid.

61. Brunner, J.S. Toward a Theory of Instruction. Cambridge, Massachusetts: Harvard University Press, 1966.

62. Joyce, Bruce R. and Beverley Showers. "Power in Staff Development Through Research on Training." A monograph for the Association for Supervision and Curriculum Development. 1983, p. 17.

63. Bacharach, Samuel B., and Sharon C. Conley. "Education Reform: A Managerial Agenda." Phi Delta Kappan, May, 1986, p. 641.

64. Joyce, Bruce R. and Beverley Showers. "Power in Staff Development Through Research on Training." A monograph for the Association for Supervision and Curriculum Development, 1983, p. 21.

65. Reese, Charley. "A guide for assessing public issues: Remember to do it on four levels." Editorial, Orlando Sentinel, July 11, 1986.

66. Barkley, Stephen G. "Coaching Teachers to Higher Levels of Effectiveness." East Windsor School District, New Jersey, July, 1987.

67. Hunter, Madeline, interview. Educational Leadership, February, 1985. p. 114.

68. Joyce, Bruce R. and Beverley Showers. "Power in Staff Development Through Research on Training."

69. Holtzman, Gary. "Establishing a Climate for Successful Teacher Coaching."

70. Joyce, Bruce R. and Beverley Showers. "Power in Staff Development Through Research on Training."

71. Ibid.

72. 1986 A.S.C.D. Yearbook. Association for Supervision and Curriculum Development, 1986.

73. Doyle, W. and G. Ponder. "The Practicality Ethic and Teacher Decision-making." Interchange, 1977. 8(3), 1-12.

74. DeBevoise, Wynn. "Collegiality May Be the Password to Effective Inservice Programs."

75. Sadler, D. Royce. "Follow-up Evaluation of an Inservice Programme Based on Action Research: Some Methodological Issues."

76. "No Recipe for Expert Teaching, Experts on Teaching Declare." ASCD Update, May, 1987.

77. Wood, Fred H. and Steven R. Thompson. "Guidelines for Better Staff Development." Educational Leadership, Feb., 1980. 37(5), 374-378. ERIC ED EJ216054 EA512457.

78. Munro, Mary Jeanne. "Effective Teacher Behaviors as an Avenue to Enhance the Self-Esteem of Teachers." Paper presented at an Inservice held at Cholla High School, Tucson, Arizona, Sept., 1982: ERIC ED 228 162.

79. Wood, Fred H. "Mining Good Staff Development Ideas in Business." NCR Corporation, Dayton, Ohio.

80. Csikszentmihalyi, Mihaly and Jane McCormack. "The Influence of Teachers." Phi Delta Kappan, February, 1986. 67(6), 415-419.

81. Ibid.

82. Berliner, David C. "On the Expert Teacher" Educational Leadership, October, 1986.

83. Ibid.

84. "Merit Pay." Research Action Brief #15, ERIC Clearinghouse on Educational Management, Eugene, OR, Feb., 1981: ERIC ED 199 828.

85. Burden, Paul R. "Professional Development as a Stressor." Phoenix, AZ, Paper presented at the Annual Meeting of the Association of Teacher Educators, Feb., 1982: ERIC ED 218 263.

86. Ibid.

87. Ibid.

88. Ibid.

89. Smith, Othanel B. "Research Bases for Teacher Education." Phi Delta Kappan, June, 1985, 687.

90. Ibid.

91. Fogarty, Joan L. and others. "A Descriptive Study of Experienced and Novice Teachers' Interactive Instructional Decision Processes." Pittsburgh, PA, Paper presented at the Annual Meeting of the American Educational Research Association, March, 1982: ERIC ED 216 007.

92. Feldvebel, Alexander H. "Teacher Evaluation: Ingredients of a Credible Model." <u>Clearing House</u>, May, 1980. 53(9), 415-420. EJ 229 375.

93. Marlow, Ediger. "Appraising the Evaluators." Missouri, Position Paper, April 4, 1983: ERIC ED 230 568.

94. Nickerson, Neal C. "Merit Pay — Does It Work in Education?" <u>NASSP Bulletin</u>, March, 1984. 68(470), 65-66. EJ 294 987.

95. Adkins, Gary A. "Pros and Cons and Current Status of Merit Pay in the Public Schools." West Virginia, Paper presented at the Annual Meeting of the West Virginia Association of Teacher Educators, Nov., 1983: ERIC ED 162.

96. Smith, B. Othanel. "Research Bases for Teacher Education."

97. Barker, Sheridan. "America's Need for Better Equipped Teachers in the Next Generation." Conference, The Challenge of Educational Reform: Seeking Solutions Cooperatively. Wilkes College, Wilkes-Barre, Pennsylvania. April, 1987.

98. "Teacher Education: The Move Toward Quality." <u>Focus</u>, 1982. p. 23.

99. <u>A Nation Prepared: Teachers for the 21st Century</u>, Carnegie Forum on Education and the Economy. Report of the Task Force on Teaching as a Profession, May, 1986.

100. <u>Reconnecting Youth</u>, Education Commission of the States, Digest of Education Statistics, 1983-85. 1985.